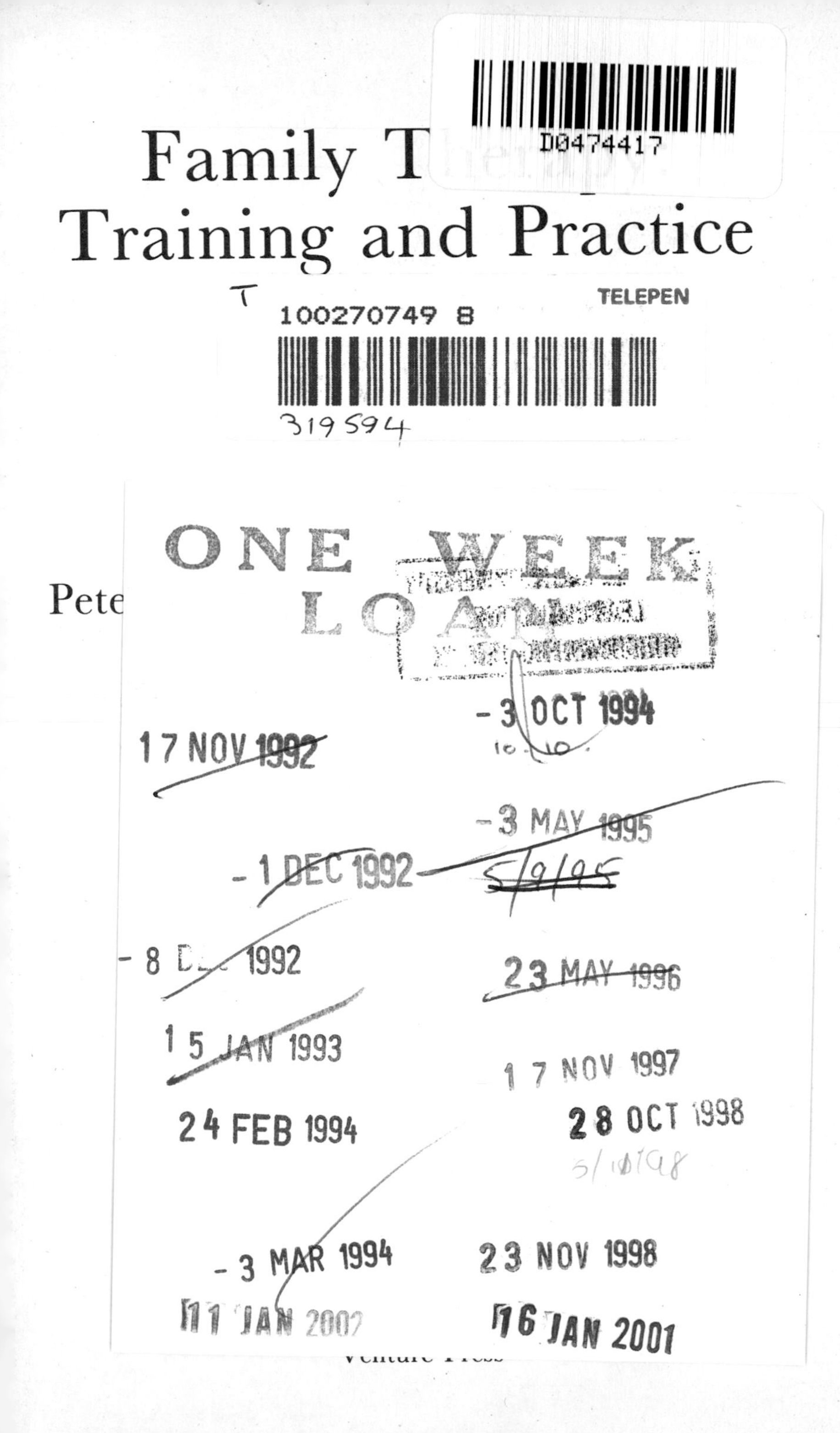

Family T
Training and Practice

Pete

Venture Press
16 Kent Street
Birmingham
B5 6RD

First published 1990

Design and production by Saxon Publishing Consultants Limited
Typeset in 10/11 Baskerville by TecSet Limited

Printed and Bound in Great Britain by
Hartnolls Limited, Bodmin, Cornwall.

ISBN 0 90010 2 802

Contents

Acknowledgements		1
Introduction		3
Chapter 1	Overview of a Systems Approach to Families and Family Therapy	7
Chapter 2	Families	15
Chapter 3	Getting Started	29
Chapter 4	Hypothesising and Circular Questioning – Defining the Problem	41
Chapter 5	Process Interventions	59
Chapter 6	Bridging Interventions	71
Chapter 7	Therapist's Tools	82
Chapter 8	Supervision	96
Section 2	Specialist Issues	107
Chapter 9	Beyond the Clinical Setting	109
Chapter 10	Close Encounters in and between Professional Systems	118
Chapter 11	A Systems View of Child Abuse	131
Chapter 12	Extending the Effectiveness of Systemic Family Therapy	140

Bibliography 149

Index 155

Acknowledgements

Our book is about family therapy practice: how to work in a systemic way with families, and how to teach and acquire these skills. Like many contemporary family therapists, our practice and teaching has been influenced by the work and tuition of, and personal contact with, Luigi Boscolo and Gianfranco Cecchin, two of the original members of the Milan Team. We have also benefitted from consultations given to the team at Leeds Family Therapy and Research Centre by Peter Lang, Principal of the Kensington Consultation Centre; Peter Bruggen, Consultant Psychiatrist, Hill End Adolescent Unit; and the Family Team, School and Family Service, Shipley, West Yorkshire, especially Larry Anderson and Kate Stewart.

A systems approach to family therapy is a continuously evolving practice paradigm. Our approach is, therefore, changing as it is 'perturbed' by contact with the work, thinking and training of other therapists whose contribution we acknowledge here. Finally, importantly, we must acknowledge the contribution of our team colleagues, past and present, but especially those who have collaborated with us in developing our training programme around which this book has evolved: Dick Agass, Dorothy Heard, and Gill Tagg.

Peter Stratton, Michael Preston-Shoot and Helga Hanks

Introduction

This book is about learning: acquiring skills in family therapy practice. It is also about teaching: communicating the core concepts and skills of this approach to practice in a manner which enables students to develop and retain a sense of their applicability and feasibility. This, then, is a book for practitioners and trainers, a book not just to be read but to be used as a basis for practice and for teaching practice. It provides a framework for thinking and analysing practice. It provides a framework for action.

The book has grown out of courses that have been run by the Leeds Family Therapy and Research Centre (LFTRC) over many years. The unique constitution of the LFTRC means that the ideas and methods that we offer here have been tried and tested in many different ways. As a working clinic, which came into existence in 1979 to acquire and develop better methods of working with families, our focus has always been on using the best available practice, extending it and providing training in a wide range of contexts. Our research activities, which have been an intrinsic component of the Centre, have enabled us to develop an understanding of family functioning and of the workings of systemic family therapy that we believe to be unique. Finally the continuity that comes from the fact that two of the authors were founder members of LFTRC and the third joined in the early years, ensures that all of this experience could be brought to bear for the benefit of this book.

Our intention has been to be intensely practical, but we would not be holding true to our methods if we did not include understanding as the basis of practicality. The whole basis of our approach is that families become stuck through clinging to particular ways of understanding each other, their relationships and the outside world. Therapy proceeds by helping them to take on alternative ways of understanding (without necessarily relinquishing their existing beliefs). Our intention is that families should leave us not just with some specific problem resolved but with an extended knowledge and outlook that will help them to cope with completely different problems in the future: and what applies to families applies equally to family therapists – you might re-read the last three sentences substituting therapists and training for families and therapy respectively.

This then is the approach we have taken in the book. We want to offer you new ways of understanding and new stories, to add to your present competence. We have no interest at all in peddling a set of tricks which will work in specific circumstances but leave you no better off if the context changes. In many ways the fact that we are presenting a systemic view makes this task much easier. The whole point of a systemic approach is that it is a general formulation which can incorporate various kinds of specific information. Furthermore, the techniques that have developed within this approach to family therapy are such that their implications are directly available. We have therefore been able to proceed very quickly to practicalities, letting the understanding develop as we go along.

One other thing that we have not done is that we have not started with a series of compelling examples of successful family therapy followed by detailed accounts of why this is *the* method of choice in almost any circumstances. Our view is that the systemic approach to understanding families makes a lot of obvious sense, and the methods work. If you have decided that you are interested in family therapy then the thing to do is to get on as quickly as possible to acquiring a preliminary understanding of the approach and then proceed to practising the techniques. We hope that you will find, as we have done, that past and current experiences suddenly make much more sense and that feelings of frustration and helplessness about difficult situations are rapidly replaced with new ideas about what could be done, and maybe even an eagerness to go and try them out.

We have organised the book in two parts. In Section 1 we present the basic concepts, techniques and core skills in family therapy, several of which were developed by the Milan team, with examples and exercises to illustrate and facilitate the introduction and use of theoretical ideas, and to provide a solid base of technique. We suggest that readers follow the sequence of the book and that trainers plan their tuition time around the chapters and the concepts they introduce. We have clearly divided the text so that it is apparent where we suggest that readers stop to undertake the exercises or tasks. This will provide a framework for learning and training.

In Section 2 we apply these concepts and skills. Here, as our main focus, we have taken child abuse, because of its centrality to much of the practice of social welfare and health agencies. However, it is our experience that family therapy is applicable to families with a wide variety of problems and challenges.

Some of the exercises are role-plays. Here we would remind readers of the importance of de-roling once the simulation exercise has been concluded. This involves each participant saying who they are not; who they are; the differences between the role they were playing and themselves; and, where appropriate, what they will be moving onto next. The purpose of this is to avoid participants taking away with them feelings and roles associated with the simulation exercise. We would also suggest that trainers should work in pairs, at least, with one trainer focusing on task and one providing a meta view on the exercises and the dynamics within them. This is because people may become distressed, either by the role they are asked to play and/or by the links this may have with their own scripts, issues and experiences, past and present. The meta position may help the trainer engaged in the task not to become enmeshed. Finally, it is our experience that people can be very nervous about role-play. Role-play provides experience, and therefore information, about being family members and therapists (Israelstam, 1988). It offers practice experience and feedback from peers and 'family members'. As such, it can facilitate the development of confidence through trying out new ideas and consolidating on experience. Nonetheless, these advantages will only become apparent if trainers have undertaken the exercises themselves, and enabled the development of sufficient trust in the group for people to 'take risks'. As with families and organisations, a balance has to be struck between, and awareness maintained, of task and process/relationship issues.

How To Use This Book

We have written this book with the clear intention that it should be used actively by people who are acquiring family therapy skills. The book is therefore addressed to the person in training and is structured on the the assumption that the many exercises will be done at the time they are offered. We do not expect that simply reading the book will be very useful. Beyond this, we hope that the book will be a flexible and versatile resource. Just one caution, if you are using the book outside of a structured training environment, we would urge you to take seriously the comments made about the importance of supervision in Chapter 8. For anyone using the book as the basis for practice or a structured course, we would recommend that they read the section on evaluation at the end of Chapter 12 so that it may be built into their plans from the start. The various ways we have in mind for the book to be used are:

1) By an individual who has some training in family therapy and who wants to refresh and extend their skills and understanding. Many of the exercises can be done by one person and some of the others will have figured in a similar form in other training. There are however several reasons why individual practice cannot be fully satisfactory, and if you are in this position, we would urge you to seek out a partner.

2) By two people who have some training, perhaps who work together, and who want to develop their abilities. Most of the exercises can be done in some form by two people, and the training will be particularly useful if the two can work as a team as they start to implement the ideas in their practice.

3) By training courses. This is likely to be the most common use. The advantage that the book offers to experienced trainers is that it provides a coherent progression in which all of the exercises needed for the development of the trainee's skills are integrated. Many of the exercises can be undertaken during the periods between

training sessions so that the contact time can be used most productively. We have found that a series of six one day workshops, at monthly intervals, is an effective vehicle for a basic level of training – perhaps it is not surprising that much of our therapy takes this form as well, though the families get much less than a full day. Of course we are not suggesting that six days are enough to train a family therapist, but that the material of Section 1 can be covered to the extent that a trainee with a good basic training in therapeutic skills, and experience of working with families, could take it away and develop it in a supportive setting, after such a course.

Each of the chapters in Section 2 would be suitable material for a one-day workshop, so a 10 day course would complete the book, but only a group that was already quite experienced should tackle the second Section without a period of practice in which to consolidate the basic techniques.

4) By experienced trainers who may wish to use the material selectively to incorporate into their courses.

5) By mutual training groups. Groups of practitioners, who work together to consult to families, could use the book for mutual training. Indeed, the origins of the LFTRC and of many other family therapy institutions that became established before there was any formal training available, suggest that a mutual training model can be very effective.

6) As a reference. The book is not intended to work as a source of reference when you first acquire it. The various sections are too interdependent, and one of our more important objectives is to build up a systemic understanding and competence in a coherent incremental way. The result is that looking up a topic in isolation is likely to be unrewarding. However, once you have worked through the book, each of the topics should have acquired a rich meaning, and it will then be possible to use it for repeated reference as you progressively acquire experience.

We have always found that teaching family therapy is stimulating, enjoyable, and rewarding. We have had a similar experience in writing this book, and hope that however you manage to use it, you will be able to share our enjoyment and have fun.

Chapter 1

Overview of a Systems Approach to Families and Family Therapy

We would like to start by introducing some people who will be with us throughout this book. They each have a problem, and it is their problem that we learn most about when we first meet them.

Celia is a neat, alert, woman of about 40 who is concerned about her family. She has no positive communication with her husband who is partly deaf and whose hearing aid never works properly, though she has the job of coping with all of the communication between them and the children. Her oldest has left home and the second has been caught up with taking drugs. The two younger girls are subdued and unhappy. For some time she has been having an affair. She feels very bad about this, but gets so little from her family that she does not want to give it up.

George is a rather gaunt looking man with a vaguely uncared for appearance. He holds down a job as a foreman, but he has for many years been drinking heavily. He does not see himself as an alcoholic, but is worried about the amount of time he has to take off from his job, and indicates that he has violent outbursts of temper both at work and within his family. Once engaged in discussion he becomes animated and cheerful, but readily lapses back into silence.

Jill, who is 14, turns up dressed entirely in black. She has been referred via her school because of her 'uncontrollable behaviour'. She is said to be promiscuous, and it appears she spends nights away from her home without telling her parents where she is. The major complaint of the school is that she collects a group of girls in the toilets where they smoke and drink alcohol. It is known that this group bring cider to school but recently Jill turned up with a bottle of brandy. Later she was found unconscious on the school bus.

The problems that George, Celia, and Jill have are not unusual, and with appropriate help, each of them may manage to find a better way to run their lives. However we get a very rapid insight into the nature of each of their problems once we realise that they are members of one family. Jill is the third child of Celia and George. Her brother has been successfully treated for his addiction, and is in the process of finding a flat to move out of the family. This will make her the oldest child living at home, with her father, with whom she no longer tries to communicate, and her mother, who has become preoccupied with her life outside of the home. Celia's lover is one of those 'secrets' that families have, meaning that everyone knows about it but nobody is allowed to mention it.

The idea of a systemic approach to families is to recognise that the way people behave, and the problems they have, develop within the context of the people and things that surround them. Families are best understood in this light. For most people, most of the time, the major influence is their family. The amount of time spent together week by week, the relative stability of the family over long periods, and the personal nature of interactions, ensure that their family, past and present, shows through powerfully in the patterns of adjustment that individuals make.

Many years of working together to help families with their difficulties have convinced us that, if anything, we still tend to underestimate the importance of families both in understanding the problems with which individuals present, and as a resource to help us in our attempts to change things.

In some ways, the behaviour of George, Jill, and Celia Calderdale is incomprehensible. Why does George cut himself off from contact by drinking heavily, aggressive outbursts and by not using his hearing aid? Why does Celia have an affair which threatens both her family and her religious principles, both of which are much more important to her than the relationship? And above all, why does Jill get herself into such situations of extreme risk, in ways that she finds distressing and not at all enjoyable? We have no easy answers, but as we work through the book, using the Calderdale family, among others, to illustrate our approach to families, we expect to produce much clearer answers than could be obtained by considering each of them in isolation.

Already we could come up with some ideas. Celia is trapped between George and the children. Both sides depend entirely on her, and yet neither is giving her anything. If she fails to mediate well enough, then George may become violent if frustrated, or just switch off completely if he is not kept adequately engaged. In order to keep things on a level basis with George, she must not make strong alliances with the children. While the children were dependent she could maintain a warm motherly relationship, but this is now only possible with Angela, the youngest. In this situation, life for Celia is a solid grind, with no sources of enjoyment or esteem from within the family so it is not too surprising that she has sought these essentials outside. It does not look as if the solution for Celia is through being helped to reconcile herself to the situation. In fact, it seems unlikely that any worthwhile solution will be achieved by her on her own: that would just be to duplicate the existing problem. What we mean here is that Celia's problem is that everyone in the family depends on her to do what is necessary, and this is what has given rise to her impossible position. To work with her on taking further responsibility and initiatives to solve the problem is to put ourselves into the same unreasonable position as the rest of the family. The outcome could be that she would finally decide it is too much and abandon both us and the family.

This is far from being a complete account of Celia's position, but already it contains some important systemic principles. First, that in a complex situation, anything that is done to change one aspect will have consequences for all the others. In terms of Celia's problems, it is easy to think of simple solutions to any one of them, but from the description above, it is clear that every simple way of reducing one problem is also a simple way of making at least two other problems worse. Furthermore, it is helpful in understanding Celia's view if we accept that she is doing the best she can in this situation. She does not regard having an affair as a good thing, but in her desperation, it seems to be the only way she can acquire the strength to carry on in the family. We will encounter this particular perspective later under the heading of 'positive connotation'. Positive connotation is a way of consistently approaching situations with the intention of understanding what it is about the actions that people have undertaken that makes them the best they could manage.

Positive connotation is nothing like saying that everything that happens is wonderful. If Johnny regularly defecates on the carpet we are not in the business of telling the family how lucky they are to have this wonderful experience. On the other hand, neither are we in the business of joining any of them in saying that this 'just proves what a sub-human specimen Johnny is.' If a person wants to obtain gratification from the inferiority of another, they will be interested in the details of that person's failures and the harm they do. This is a clue to the fact that if we want to get past this (often very tempting) response, we must find a different strategy. Positive connotation is tied up with trying to understand how, in their confusion and desperation, the person could think of nothing more useful. The final result may be undesirable to them and everybody else, and they may be pushed into claiming that they could not help it, but again this is a perception that we would want to avoid as far as possible. So positive connotation is tied up with some fundamental aspects of our approach, and we hope to enrich the concept as we work through this book. For now, what we want to stress is the extra room for manoeuvre that we obtain by positively connoting rather than disparaging or blaming.

Returning to Celia, making a judgement about her immorality, weakness, or foolishness will not usually get us very far in helping to change the situation. Telling people they are immoral does not tend to make them feel good, and eager to ally with you in a positive attack on the problem. Also it rather sets you up for thinking that if the problem is their lack of morals, the solution must be to increase their morals. We want to get results much more quickly and easily than by taking on the job of putting morals into people. The same applies to weakness, foolishness and, of course, madness. In fact the point is very general: it is often easy to see that if only a certain person was different, then there would be no problem. But priests, politicians, and psychoanalysts have all found that changing people is extraordinarily difficult. So the answer may look simple, but it is almost impossible to achieve. This is why the systemic approach is so attractive.

Although it seems more complex to have to take account of what the rest of Celia's family is doing, in practice we find that it makes bringing about change very much easier. So we are not denying the validity of descriptions of people, and we are not claiming that individual characteristics do not account for much of behaviour. What we are saying is that individual accounts are only one partial perspective, and we can bypass the dead ends that the perspective tends to produce by taking a systemic view.

Incidentally it is worth pointing out that families do very often account for unwanted behaviour in terms of the characteristics of individuals. 'If only you weren't so bossy' or 'if only you were like Jane' are very common 'solutions' that have no chance whatsoever of causing any change. One useful systemic guideline is that if you find you are proposing the same solution that the family already believes in, the chances are that you are completely stuck.

We now propose an exercise. As it is the first in the book, we will describe the procedure in some detail. Subsequent exercises will assume you have completed this one, so general instructions will not be repeated.

Exercise 1.1 (30 minutes)
All exercises are headed in this way, numbered within chapters and with an estimate of the time it will take. These times are based on our experience but we know that there is great variability in how long they take. Our strategy is always to build in a substantial extra margin, which can be used for group discussion if needed.

The exercise is for the full group. [Even with two people it could be done in some form, and one person could imagine the variety of responses that the exercise might produce. As with other exercises, many adaptations are possible, and we intend them to be used with ingenuity.] The group is to listen to two pieces of music. Suggestions, which the person running the exercise should look at, are provided at the end of this chapter. After the first piece, each person is to write down the psychiatric condition that the piece most makes them think of, then they are to list the emotions that they feel are portrayed in the music.

After the second piece, just list the emotions.

Finally the group should spend 10 minutes comparing the psychiatric condition, and the moods that individuals have come up with.

Two final technical points: the most important is that the exercises are clearly ruled off from the rest of the text and all instructions for an exercise that you should complete before reading further will be contained between the two rules; and any notes pertaining to that exercise are marked thus: *. Reading on without doing the exercise is likely to significantly reduce the benefit you get from it when you eventually do it. So we would strongly suggest that you try very hard to do the exercises as they appear. The second point is that when information is provided for only some of the people in an exercise it is put at the end of the chapter. In this case, we felt that the discussion of titles of music might provide a set that would make it more difficult for you to have your own ideas, so we have put the titles out of the way.

Thinking about the exercise, our experience is that in any group, there is always at least one alternative psychiatric condition offered in response to the first piece of music; and there is also a good variety of moods offered for each piece. It would have been possible to have had a discussion of whose judgement is correct, and this kind of discussion is more likely over the psychiatric condition. With the moods, groups more naturally assume that alternative perceptions may be legitimate. Consider how your group discussion went. There is usually some tendency to think just in terms of the effect of the music on different individuals. We want to suggest a way of looking at the differences between individuals that goes beyond this. The perception of a mood is something created between an individual and the music: it is not a property of just one or the other, but a result of putting the two together. Whatever emotions you as an individual produced, it would be possible for you to accept different feelings that other people in the group proposed, and use these to obtain a much richer response when you hear the music again.

The general point here is that when we perceive a complex reality, the meaning that emerges is not a property of the external object, and it is not something just inside us. It is created (we tend to say co-created) between us and the reality. Giving up the idea of perception as being a kind of picture, more or less accurate, of reality, enables us to recognise that there may be many alternative perceptions. Furthermore it is not the case that one is correct and the others are wrong. Now we can see that when our perceptions are not helping us, it may be possible to find an alternative perspective to lay alongside the view we already have. In this way we can enrich our understanding, and open up new possibilities for action.

Although we reject the idea of one perspective being true and the others false, we do not see all perceptions as equally useful. If you were going to have to listen to the first piece of music frequently and you hear it as irritatingly smug and jolly in a highly superficial way, your perceptions would have unfortunate consequences. You would be prevented from hearing any of the subtleties, and you would become increasingly distressed at being exposed to it. If you could accept several of the other suggestions made by members of your group, you would be provided with alternative ways of reacting to the music and, most importantly, some choice about how to respond to it. Much of family therapy is about unhooking people from the idea that they have the truth and others are wrong. This is a complex idea which goes under names like 'social constructivism'. We will enrich the concept as we progress through the book.

You may like to know that if you have read this far, you have already encountered many of the important principles of the systemic approach. The reason that you hardly felt a thing is that the principles are not in fact mysterious, amazingly novel or difficult to grasp. Most of them we already use in one form or another, but there is one feature that does make the systemic approach unique. This is, that we try to distinguish good systemic ideas that will make our work easier, from habitual patterns of thinking (for example, blaming the person for whom things have gone wrong) which may make our task impossible. Then we try to be extremely consistent in applying these methods and avoiding slipping into the old ways of thinking. So throughout this book we will be asking you to use systemic thinking as consistently and rigorously as you can. Sometimes we will even be asking you to exaggerate the systemic approach until you can get the hang of it, after which you will be able to settle back into a more relaxed style.

The time has come to explain what a systems approach to family therapy is and where it came from. This book is rigorously practical, so this section is short, but we will refer to publications that will enable you to take the issues further if you wish.

The Origins of a Systems Approach to Family Therapy

After the second world war a group of quite extraordinary scientists assembled at the Macy Institute. Some had been working on guided missiles during the war and all of them were fascinated by the way that electronics had allowed the construction of goal directed machines. The underlying phenomenon was that of negative feedback. As this concept is fundamental to all systems, we will begin with it.

A goal seeking machine can be very simple. It requires some kind of sensor to indicate how far it is from its goal. Then it needs some process which will move it in relation to the goal. If it operates according to negative feedback, information that the distance from the goal is increasing will make it change its behaviour; information that it is getting closer to the goal will make it maintain its behaviour. A fair example is provided by the children's game of 'getting warmer'. One child is blindfolded and moves about randomly. The rest shout 'getting colder' if the move is away from the goal, and 'getting warmer' if the move is towards it. Usually the seeker will end up in contact with the goal, though anyone who has played the game as a child will tell you that the system is not perfect!

When the seeker fails to reach the target, we have an illustration of why simple systems can get stuck. If the target is in the next room, then you get warmer until you are up against the wall. To get to the target you have to move away from it, and towards the door, which is beyond the capacity of a system controlled by simple negative feedback. Families too, are sometimes trapped by having responses which make things a little better but which, in fact, move them further away from a solution. They are showing goal seeking behaviour which moves them closer to their goal, and so gives the illusion of progress, but only down a blind alley. Under intense stress and unhappiness it seems we all have a strong tendency to revert to this simple kind of functioning.

Another common example is the thermostat in an electric circuit that sets a boiler going. If the temperature rises above the setting, the circuit will be interrupted, the boiler will shut off and the temperature will fall. If the temperature drops below the acceptable range the thermostat will complete the circuit and the boiler will come on, again reducing the distance from the goal.

In these examples the feedback is called negative because it works to reduce the distance from the goal. Positive feedback also exists, and here it is movement away from the goal that amplifies the movement. This is not what we usually want; imagine a thermostat that was wired in reverse. The colder it got the more the boiler would be switched off, and the hotter it got the more the boiler would put out heat. Eventually the boiler would be either permanently on or permanently off, and the system would reach a temperature limit determined by external constraints. A very familiar example of positive feedback in action is a sound system in which the speakers feed directly into the microphone. Perhaps you can already see that many processes within families could usefully be viewed as strong negative feedback which keeps the options rigidly limited, or positive feedback that results in rapid escalation of any tendency (called 'runaway') so that it either hits external limits or self-destructs.

The group of scientists at the Macy Institute that we referred to earlier were excited by the possibility of applying their ideas to biological phenomena. Fairly quickly, the brain became the biological system of most interest and systems ideas began to be applied to human functioning. Because of the interest in dysfunction, a group started to explore the application of systems ideas to psychiatric symptoms. Gregory Bateson was the leading figure in a group that set up in Palo Alto, California to research issues of communication with the new ideas, and this group started to study schizophrenia. Almost accidentally they happened to observe one or two of their patients with the rest of their families and, suddenly, behaviour that had appeared bizarre and incomprehensible began to make sense. This was probably the point at which a systemic understanding of the family began and from here the history is rich and complex. We will not explore it in detail because there is already an excellent account provided by Hoffman (1981), and an overview of the insights of the Palo Alto group is provided in another superb book by Watzlawick, Beavin and Jackson (1967). These two books will enable you to obtain an idea of the excitement, the usefulness, and the range of ideas in systemic family therapy. Here we would just mention two routes that family therapy has taken that have grown out of, and to some extent away from, the Palo Alto approach. Salvador Minuchin (1974) developed an approach (called structural family therapy) based on rearranging family structure, in particular, the routes of communication and generational boundaries that structure the workings of families. Another group developed what has become known as strategic family therapy in which the emphasis is on using any tactics that might produce the wanted kind of change in the family. A useful account of the work of this group, which has the added advantage of showing how the approach can be used in working with individuals, is the book by Fisch, Weakland and Segal (1982).

For our history we will now jump to Milan and a group of psychiatrists grouped around Mara Selvini Palazzoli. Palazzoli discovered the Palo Alto work in the later sixties, and a group of (until then) psychoanalytically oriented psychiatrists came together to develop methods of family therapy based particularly on Bateson's writings (see Bateson, 1973). After a decade in which they worked particularly with families with an anorexic member, the original group published their major book (Selvini Palazzoli, Boscolo, Cecchin, and Prata, 1978). Soon after, Luigi Boscolo and Gianfranco Cecchin undertook a substantial programme of travel around the world to offer training in their methods. The Milan Associates continued to develop their methods. The original team split up and have pursued rather different routes.

You will encounter 'Milan methods' throughout this book because they have been the major influence on the work of the Leeds Family Therapy and Research Centre (LFTRC) since 1981. The techniques that we have developed, and that we teach, owe a very great debt especially to Boscolo and Cecchin. That being the case, we will not attempt to summarise their ideas here, but get straight on with our first task which is to lay the foundations for a systemic understanding of families.

Appendix

Materials for Exercise 1.1

We have run this exercise using 'The Arrival of the Queen of Sheba' for the first piece, and a gaelic folk song for the second (it is an advantage when nobody in the group speaks gaelic). Alternatives could be the mazurka from Act 1 of Coppelia by Delibes, and the first movement of the film score for Alexander Nevsky by Prokofiev (called 'Russia Under the Yoke of the Mongolians'), which we have found effective in mood induction experiments. The precise choice of music is not important. These examples should give you an idea of what is needed. If it is really impossible to provide music, the exercise could be done using appropriate pictures.

Chapter 2

Families

Our goal in this chapter is to build up an understanding of how families work, but families are made up of people, and we want to start with some observations about basic aspects of individual functioning. Our starting point is that people are continually adapting to their context as they perceive it. So of course do cats, goldfish and all other living organisms. These adaptations are often subtle and ingenious, but they are also often unconscious. They may result from processes such as physiological reactions of which we have no awareness; they may be so practised that we do not notice them any more; or there may be powerful psychological processes operating to keep them out of conscious awareness. Because adaptations are not usually carefully considered, with all of the implications thought through (there are just too many for that) they are often in the form of a short-term solution to the obvious and immediate demands. In other words, they can be very short-sighted and based on a narrow perspective. This is particularly true when the person is under stress. The nature of adaptation, and its roles in relationships, is explored in the context of babies and their caregivers by Stratton (1982).

A basic factor in any individual's adaptation is their perception of the world. Family therapy has enthusiastically adopted the idea that there is no fixed external reality which we perceive more or less accurately. Rather, we each construct our own unique world, largely through our relationships and interactions. So each person's understanding of the world, and of each specific event, is unique, and it is not meaningful to ask whether or not it is true. It is, though, worth asking whether the perception is functional. If John encounters a group of young men and perceives them as thugs who are out to mug him, his behaviour will produce a reaction from them. Between them they will construct what happens next. More informatively, since they are doing it between them, we can talk of John and the young men 'co-

constructing' their reality. The important point is that, moment by moment, particularly in social contexts, we create what happens through the interactions of our expectations and the expression of these in our behaviour.

It is difficult to accept that what we know is just one version of many possible realities, and it is something that we will have to work at throughout this book. The idea has a respectable history, and useful though not particularly easy accounts are provided in Shotter and Gergen (1989) and Segal (1986). One relevant individual tendency is that we are extremely alert to causal connections, and families spend much time producing explanations of each other's behaviour. The theme of causality runs throughout this book, but a fundamental process that you might start looking for in the examples is the way that causality may be reversed. Most commonly, a family will say that the symptom is the cause of their problems. Our task very often is to persuade them to accept that it is also possible to think of the problems making the symptom necessary.

Exercise 2.1 (20 minutes)
We would like you to take 5 minutes to produce a short list of some behaviours or feelings of your own which you might prefer to do without, but which you feel you cannot help. To make this easier to do, choose a person who knows you really well, and imagine which of your behaviours and feelings they would put in this category. Keep the list but do not show it to anyone. To continue the exercise, take each item on your list in turn, and in your imagination ask the person you chose to guess what you would expect to happen if you behaved differently.

Symptoms often force people to achieve something that they could not claim to want to do. For each of the behaviours you listed, would the person you chose be able to suggest anything that it makes you do, or stops you doing that you might want, but that you would not feel free to choose to do voluntarily?

---

*Through very different methods, every form of psychological therapy is designed to give people a greater sense of control, and a greater awareness of the control they have, over their feelings and actions. Jay Haley (1963) offers a surprisingly useful definition of a symptom as: 'An extreme behaviour accompanied by the communication "I can't help it."'

*Much of what we are doing in therapy is to try to shift attention away from causal beliefs like 'I can't help it, that's the way I am' and towards the possibility of acting differently. But one of the things that prevents people from acting differently is their expectation of what would happen if they did.

Did you find, for at least some of your list, that it is not that you cannot do differently, but that up to now it has seemed better not to? In other words, you are not a helpless victim of this tendency; you have been making a choice.

Families are connected to the wider culture and society at various levels. The ways that family members understand each other are influenced by what they have learned outside the family (Stratton, 1988a). Influence is reciprocal, but one aspect that will concern us is the way that families see their own workings in terms that reflect their current perceptions of the external world. Boscolo, Cecchin, Hoffman and Penn (1987) have pointed out how the stories that the Milan therapists constructed during the 1970s, that were accepted by the families they were treating, relied heavily on cold war phraseology. Today, the group feel that even if they could think creatively in these terms, their families would not accept stories expressed in the language of ten or fifteen years ago.

Families have their own life cycle. Both the physical maturation of individuals (a process that continues throughout life) and the roles prescribed in society for families at different stages, bring inevitable change. It is these changes that prevent families from remaining in a fixed form indefinitely, but it is when change is demanded that problems in previous adjustments are most likely to become apparent. An extensive account of families understood in terms of their life cycle is given by Carter and McGoldrick (1989).

Clearly the very brief sketch provided in this chapter is far from comprehensive. Useful starting points for further ideas about how families work are: Walsh (1982), L'Abate (1985) and the special issue of the Journal of Family Therapy (Contributions to Family Therapy, Vol 10 (3), 1988).

Aspects of Families that Enable Things to go Wrong

1) *Imbalances of power*

Families, more than most situations, incorporate enormous differences in the power that individuals can wield. Superior physical strength, a greater verbal facility, or ability to manipulate emotions, or stronger religious or political conviction, or the dependency that may come from physical disability, may all be used to control the behaviour of other family members. Sometimes financial power is used that enables one person to be dominant in defining reality.

Within systemic family therapy a major disagreement has raged for many years over the issue of power. Jay Haley believes that power is fundamental in the negotiation of inter-personal relationships, while Gregory Bateson made the point that thinking of power leads one to think in terms of an attribute that some have and others haven't, and that this is misleading (Dell, 1989). Bateson's view is that power is something negotiated between people, and he offers the idea that the power of a dictator exists only because it is conferred on them by the people. As we write, events in Eastern Europe, and particularly the spectacularly sudden collapse of power once its limitations are recognised, are a clear indication of the truth in Bateson's view. But the one-sidedness with which a powerful position was exploited by such as Ceausescu makes Haley's claim undeniable. Here we have a nice example of alternative stories, each of which has value. It seems to us that it is possible to think of extreme examples to fit either view, but the more important issue is which perception is most useful for dealing with family problems. The answer will not be the same for all families, and those in which abuse occurs are particularly important here. Dell (1989) and Fish (1990) discuss the issue in some detail, but it could also make a fruitful topic for a class debate.

2) *Secrets*

Families have a powerful tendency to define topics as not to be discussed or even mentioned. This tendency enables beliefs that seem quite bizarre when they are finally expressed, to exist without being challenged. Often the belief itself is perfectly straightforward, and it is just the fact that it is defined as a secret that is damaging. For example, in one of our families the father informed us that John was adopted but that he did not know. John, who was 6 years old (and not deaf), listened to this statement without comment. He clearly knew that he was adopted, but he also knew that the important thing about this was that it was not discussed within the family.

Being able to forbid discussion enables families to play various kinds of games. When the Calderdales came to see us, the family had known for a long time that father was alcoholic, but because this was not to be mentioned, it was not possible to include the belief in any of their discussions about how the family worked. So Mrs Calderdale's worries about whether he would lose his job could not be explored and therefore could not be resolved. Also his sporadic aggression had to be attributed to frustration with his deafness, but it was clear that attempts to solve the aggression by dealing with his hearing were doomed to failure. A similar set of binds derived from the 'secret' affair that Mrs Calderdale was conducting. Family secrets are a potent source of 'unsolvable' problems.

3) *More of the same*

When things start to go wrong, there will often be a solution that solved the problem in the past. The tendency then is to assume that the answer is to apply the old solution, but more effectively – it must be done harder, longer, or whatever. This tendency is not unique to families but they do seem particularly likely to fall into it. One reason may come from the tendency of families to change over time. For stable situations, it may be true that what worked in the past is the first thing to try next time, whereas if the family has entered a new phase, this is less likely to work. However, what we really need to understand is why the 'solution' is not abandoned when it becomes a source of stress itself, and is clearly not working. As with many of these issues we find that people can often gain insight most effectively from their own experience.

Exercise 2.2 (10 minutes)
Take 5 minutes to identify a problem with which you have been struggling unsuccessfully for some time. Then list in summary all of the things you have done to try to solve it.

---

*When you review your list, the first thing to look for is whether there is any sense in which your solutions are just 'more of the same'. Are you tackling a new or changed situation by escalating the responses that worked in the past? If your list has several items, then there is another question we can ask.

*When an individual says that they have tried everything, they are usually telling the truth, but only in a very specific way. If they describe all the things they have tried, these 'solutions' can often be seen to be every possible variation of one particular solution. Albert may have been to his GP, and a psychotherapist, changed his diet, attended a group, and a faith healer, and taken homeopathic remedies, all to no avail. His family are likely to offer the list as proof of how hard he has tried, but all of his solutions are a variant on the one solution of obtaining a cure through therapy. You might examine your list and see whether there is any sense in which your different attempts are really one solution.

When such a pattern appears, we tend to assume that there is a definition of the problem which leads to this solution and no other. As if there were something safe about the existing definition, and something dangerous about thinking of an alternative. Perhaps everyone can accept that the problem is some dysfunction inside Albert, and be very active in supporting him in trying to get it fixed. To try different solutions they might have to all accept that, say, the symptoms arise because Albert hates his job. If this possibility is too threatening for everyone to consider, they are forced to look for solutions to the problem that they can accept – and they are doomed to keep trying ineffective solutions unless one of them accidentally solves the real problem.

4) *Identity*
Because families largely define each person's identity, they can be very powerful in both specifying what a person can do, and in posing a threat to the identity that the person is currently trying to establish. The result is seen in patterns of family interaction in which it seems as

if the very existence of the individuals is threatened. Over and over again we encounter people who feel they cannot change because of the effects that would have within the family. Although this is a complex phenomenon, which is partly maintained by the disposition of families to declare many topics as 'not for discussion' (above) we can identify two other relevant factors: i) no weakness; and ii) no shocks.

'No weakness' describes the resistance to giving up a behaviour which the person sees as protecting them or giving them influence within the family. In the Calderdale family, George could not give up his deafness because it might have exposed him to clear communications from his children.

'No shocks' summarises the power of expectations within the family. Somehow it is very difficult to act out of the character with which your family has endowed you while you are in their presence. If all the family expect you to be (i.e. knows for sure that you are) modest or dishonest, or competent, then at least in some cases, it seems very difficult to do anything that would invalidate that perception. If you do, as when Celia started an affair, the family will simply deny the existence of this 'impossible' event.

Both of these tendencies are tied up with the power of the family history to build up a definition of the individuals in the family, to define what behaviour is appropriate, and to specify how events are to be perceived and understood. One result is that people find that their choice of behaviour is being determined entirely by the family situation, and they feel they have no freedom to behave differently. Stratton (1988a) provides a general account of how family perceptions set up stable patterns of functioning, and how these processes relate to the relationship between the family and the wider culture.

The list of family characteristics that we have described points to recognisable and repeated patterns of family functioning. When the tendencies of individuals that we identified at the start of this chapter are combined with the unique features of families, it is possible to see why families seem to exist as objects in their own right. They seem to have their own existence and natural laws by which they operate, and individual members may often feel that the family itself has taken on life and is forcing them to behave in ways that conflict with their wishes. We now introduce some of the more important concepts developed within family therapy to provide a more specific understanding of these processes.

Beliefs

Families develop shared beliefs about the world which may be quite complex, and seem to be very persistent. Family therapy has been more concerned with unspoken beliefs, but even clearly recognised 'facts' can be very powerful. Everybody knew that George had a disposition to be violent, and they complained about it, but the belief had a powerful influence on every member of the family. Sometimes things are known but the family may not mention them to you. It may just be obvious that people always go wrong when they first leave home, and this may be a common topic of conversation within the family. But they may not want to waste the time of a busy professional in stating obvious facts. Sometimes the topic may simply fail to come up. We saw one family in which the mother, who was a frail and retiring woman, seemed to have an extraordinary hold on everyone. Later we discovered that she was a witch (literally, according to family belief). This was not a secret, it was just that nobody thought it relevant to the problem with which they had come (and we had not thought to ask), and so it was not mentioned.

Myths

Families, over the years, develop strong sets of beliefs which constitute a kind of 'inner image' of family life. Myths may take generations to build up, and they may never be clearly stated, but they tend to have the following characteristics:

1) They are shared by the whole family.
2) They exert an influence on all family members and on their relationships.
3) They go unchallenged despite the fact that they do not square with reality (Ferreira, 1963). A simple and very common myth is 'we are a happy family'. Everyone in the family knows that it is essential to maintain this belief, and so indications of unhappiness have to be classified as symptoms of illness. Arguments can be stopped rather than resolved, by recourse to the myth, and in general moves towards growth may be stultified if they contain an implicit message of dissatisfaction. We return to family myths in more detail in Chapter 7, and here move on to a related concept.

Scripts

The notion of scripts has been developed particularly by Byng-Hall (1985, 1988). Family life often has the flavour of a drama, and family therapy provides a stage for the re-enactment of familiar scenes. Family members can be thought of as having learned a script, primarily from their family of origin, which tells them what their role is and how the family play should develop in its various functions. As Byng-Hall (1986) points out, not only is every person casting the rest of the family in their inner world script, they also simultaneously are playing roles in everyone else's scripts.

Families negotiate so that scripts become compatible, and when a couple come together to set up a family, Byng-Hall (1985) identifies two kinds of script. The replicative script, which aims to repeat the past, and the corrective script which attempts to alter past experience. If both parents left home at seventeen, they may build this into their assumptions about how families work and create a family which incorporates this event in everyone's script. An over-protected child may grow up to be an adult who is determined to correct this script in their own parenting. Both kinds of script allow the past to determine the future, and lead to the same patterns being repeated over and over again. Therapists need to be alert to these repeating patterns in order to recognise the underlying script which can then be brought into the open and challenged.

Family Fixes: the Double Bind

One of the great insights of Bateson and his colleagues was to identify the process that they labelled the double bind (Sluzki and Ransom, 1976). In a double bind a person is apparently offered alternatives but in fact whatever they do will be wrong. As an example a father might forbid his son to climb a tree because it is dangerous. If the boy climbs the tree he is punished for disobedience, but if he doesn't, his father indicates that he is disappointed in him for being so soft. Whatever this boy does he is going to feel inadequate and guilty: he has done the wrong thing again and disappointed his parents. The bind does not have to be current: a man may grow up with an image of masculinity that is highly macho and a model of a good husband as being sensitive and caring. Within his marriage, any move to satisfy one definition will create problems for the other.

A double bind is not a simple contradiction. If someone tells you to stand up while sitting down you would just refuse or laugh at the ridiculousness of the request. One feature of a double bind is that it is not immediately obvious, though it is not necessarily complex nor secretive. The classic simple example is to command someone to do something spontaneously. If they don't do it they are proving they cannot be spontaneous, but if they do it, they are merely conforming which is not spontaneous at all. What makes double binds difficult to recognise is that the two demands are at different logical levels. The boy in our first example may concentrate on the behaviour being demanded and find he has failed at the level of being the wrong kind of son, or he can be the kind of boy his father appears to want but always be getting into trouble. The macho man has a concept of masculinity that is logically distinct from his concept of a good husband, and so the two can conflict without the contradiction becoming apparent.

A number of the features of individuals and families that we identified earlier in this chapter help to explain why double binds are so common in families. The most obvious is the range of needs that families meet, because these are at many different levels. So they are not only likely to conflict with each other: they may do so in a way that makes the reason for the conflict difficult to identify. A man who wants to maintain a personal identity of toughness, but who also wants to be looked after physically within the family may have to develop some odd behaviours. One solution might be to engage in sporting activities, or fights outside the pub, so that the toughness is maintained, but because of his injuries he can demand care and rest within the family.

Exercise 2.3 (25 minutes)
Consider the information you have about the Calderdale family, and identify any double binds that each of them may be experiencing. Make up groups of four to come up with suggestions for each member of the family for 15 minutes, then pool the answers in the whole group to see what variations there are.

---

*Some of our ideas are offered at the end of the chapter, but remember that we have abandoned ideas of absolute truth so they are not there for you to see if you got it right. The only reality we need to be concerned with is whether it seemed to work like this to members of the family. For that purpose all of your ideas are likely to offer useful opportunities for exploration with the family.

The identification of double binds is an essential ingredient of any attempt to understand any interpersonal situation in which a person appears to be stuck. We would therefore suggest a further exercise.

Exercise 2.4 (15 minutes)
First, list some work situations in which you do not seem to be able to get things right whatever you do. Then for each one, write down the thing you would have to do that would give the best chance of completely solving the problem. Now write next to it, the worst thing that would be likely to happen if you did it. If the bad consequence would undermine the solution, then you have probably identified a double bind.

Punctuations and circles

Our first concept here is the basis for the classic story about the three blind people trying to work out what an elephant is by feeling different parts of it. Each had a partial perspective – like a tree, a snake, a stone depending whether they were feeling a leg, the trunk, or a tusk. Such partial perspectives of a complex reality have come to be called 'punctuations' within family therapy. We tend only to notice that aspect of a complex system that is obvious and relevant to us, and that is usually the most useful way to operate. But what often happens, is that we decide our punctuation is *the* reality and then get into an argument with people who have noticed a different aspect.

Thinking back to the exercise (1.1) using two kinds of music in Chapter 1, we could see this as an example of specific punctuations.

Each perception was valid, and not in conflict with the others. Combining all of the punctuations would have given a much richer account of the pieces of music than any individual punctuation could manage. The trap is to think that if one is valid then all the others must be false, and then get into an argument over whose reality is more true.

When trying to understand a system, punctuations are likely to focus on causes. A natural reaction when we see some odd piece of behaviour is to ask what caused it. Let us take a classic example: a mother comes complaining that her 20 year old son spends all day in bed and will not do anything however hard she tries to energise him. When the two are seen the son complains that his mother nags all the time and it gets him down and makes him depressed. As we obtain descriptions of what actually happens day by day at home it becomes clear that each of them is giving an accurate description, but it is only partial. The recognition of a simple cause-effect sequence is the natural human tendency described in the first section of this chapter, and in simple situations it often serves our purposes. However in an interpersonal situation, it will almost inevitably oversimplify. These partial perspectives are called *linear punctuations*. They are a selection of one causal sequence from within a more complex situation.

It is easy to see that we could fit the two 'punctuations' together to give a fuller and more useful picture. *Figure 2.1* does this, and it comes naturally to present such combinations of causes in a circle, because each affects the other endlessly.

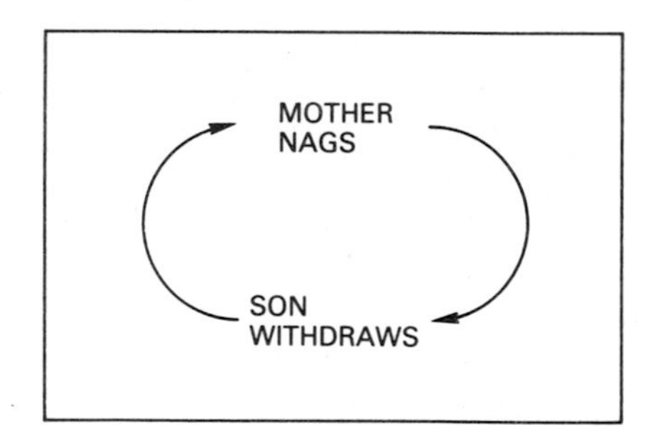

Figure 2.1 Cycle composed of two. linear causal sequences

The recognition that within families, and in most other situations in which people interact, any response of an individual is likely to become a cause in somebody's behaviour subsequently, has led to a description of these sequences as being 'transactions'. Family therapists have been particularly struck by those sequences, like our example, in which the second causal effect feeds back to start a new version of the previous cause. Situations in which there may be a great deal of activity, but nothing changes, are fundamental in systems that have got stuck, so recognising these cycles is one of the most important tasks. Because of this basic role, the image of the circle has acquired great significance within the field.

In looking at how people set up circular patterns (whether or not vicious) Gregory Bateson and his co-workers identified three kinds of common sequence. The first, labelled *symmetry* refers to sequences in which a given form of behaviour by one person produces a corresponding form from the other. If X is aggressive, Y may respond by being aggressive back. X, adopting a linear punctuation, sees aggression as an appropriate response to Ys behaviour, and so the cycle can continue indefinitely.

Complementary sequences occur when a behaviour elicits its opposite. If Y responds to Xs aggression with submissiveness, and X regards submissive behaviour as a trigger for aggression, we may again have a continuing cycle of behaviour.

Both symmetrical and complementary cycles have a tendency to continue, but they will only be stable while the responses are roughly at the same level as the one before. If the response is stronger than the preceding behaviour then we have an *escalating* sequence that will eventually get out of control: a glare produces an insult which is responded to with abuse which provokes a blow which requires a harder blow and so on. Eventually in such sequences a limit is reached: one person is incapacitated; both become exhausted; an outside influence (say a parent) intervenes; or one of the pair switches to the other kind of sequence.

In many relationships, people find it possible to switch between symmetrical and complementary responses in a way that keeps the sequence moving, but within safe limits and without either person losing out. This kind of sequence is called *reciprocal*, and can clearly be expected to be healthier.

A classic account of such sequences is given by Watzlawick, Beavin and Jackson (1967) analyzing the play *Who's afraid of Virginia Woolf?* by Edward Albee. The arguments between the couple (Richard Burton and Elizabeth Taylor in the subsequent film version) provide a rich selection of variations on these basic patterns.

Exercise 2.5 (25 minutes)
Make up groups of about seven. Set up a role-play of the Calderdales, just using the information you already have and spend 15 minutes trying to make symmetrical, complementary and reciprocal sequences happen while discussing Jill's symptoms. Have two observers for each family who will note the occurrence and discuss with the family before de-roling.

---

*From this exercise you are likely to have discovered how difficult it is to do less than the partner during each circle.

Spirals: the Development of a Problem

We now want to point out that our circle in *Figure 2.1* is itself a punctuation because it shows the state of affairs at one specific time. A fuller account would show how this circle was progressively achieved, and the three kinds of sequences that we have just considered give us a basis for this.

The cycle of nagging and withdrawal probably started out as a minor and adaptive complementary pattern. Over the years, mother had taken responsibility for her son's level of activity, and he had come to rely on her to activate him. As he entered adolescence, mother was at times concerned that he was not developing his interests, but had some ambivalence about him becoming too independent and eventually leaving her: a double bind of wanting him to achieve but not wanting to lose him. So she put pressure on him to do things, but in a way that attributed his lack of activity to his character. So the son was being told that he could not do things on his own initiative, and there was a history to support this belief. By now he is beginning to find the pressure uncomfortable and to try to avoid it by staying out of mother's way, usually by staying in bed until late every morning. But a strengthening claim that his failure to activate himself was due to his constitution, could rapidly become a pattern of blaming which would reduce his self-esteem and reinforce the idea that he is helpless to change things for himself. So both become stressed, and react by escalating their efforts until we have the circular pattern which uses up all of their energy.

Symptoms as Solutions

The first idea we introduced in this chapter was our tendency to adapt to situations, in a rather short-sighted way, as we encounter them. One of the most fundamental aspects of the systemic perspective is to assume that attempts to adapt, and to solve a problem, lie at the origins of the problems with which families present. However bizarre, distressing, and destructive a symptom may be, it almost certainly started life as somebody's attempt to resolve a problem within the family. In our *Figure 2.2* example, putting extra pressure on her son to mobilise him was the most obviously useful thing that the mother could think of. Trying to maintain his relationship with his mother by minimising the impact of her nagging was a natural response for the boy. But these solutions did nothing to resolve more fundamental problems, and so both partners did 'more of the same', escalating their attempts in a direct response to their diminishing effectiveness.

For now we just want to make a claim, and ask you to consider it as a possibility. As we progress through descriptions of how this approach to family therapy works, we hope that this idea will gradually acquire meaning. The suggestion is that every symptom started life as the solution to a problem. In order to understand why a family or an individual is behaving in a damaging and distressing way, it will be very much more helpful to understand how this behaviour is the end product of the kinds of processes sketched out in this chapter, than to dismiss them as crazy or evil.

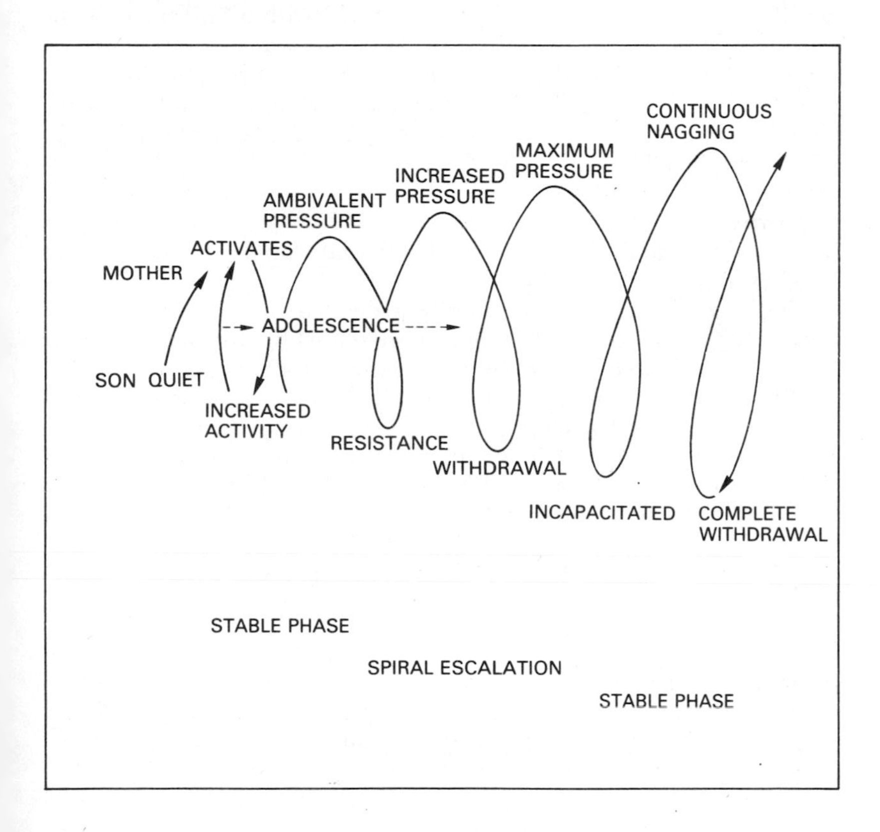

Figure 2.2 A spiral to produce the circle of Figure 2.1

One final piece of jargon for the present. When a solution is carried over into a new situation, in which it is no longer effective, it is seen as being *redundant*. If you see someone walking down the street dressed as Napoleon you might be tempted to make assumptions about their mental state. Discovering that their car broke down on the way back from a fancy dress party enables you to see that the clothing is not an inappropriate response to your neighbourhood but a left-over or redundant solution to some other situation. One of the repeated positive experiences of systemic family therapy is the discovery that what had looked like crazy or wicked behaviour is just a redundant solution, perceived out of context.

Conclusion

In this chapter we have described the common, and rather ordinary processes, through which families sometimes get into difficulties from which they then find it very difficult to escape. When they arrive for family therapy we are, of course, confronted with a late stage in the process, and the task is to understand how they reached this point. By using the ideas in this chapter, we hope to make it possible to do this while maintaining respect for and empathy with all members of the family. Now it is time to find out how the first stages of family therapy can be handled.

Appendix

Some possible double binds in the Calderdale family, to add to ideas from Exercise 2.3.

The religious values of the family presented the children with the injunction to be good like their parents while the parents were aggressive, alcoholic, and having extra-marital affairs.

Both Jack and Jill at different times were indicating that they wanted and needed to be looked after, but were having their problems in situations where the parents could not protect them.

Father was being told that he should sort his hearing aid out but simultaneously the children made sure he could not hear them.

Chapter 3
Getting Started

Practitioners and agencies work out their own ways of handling referrals. This chapter presents one approach to working with referrals, and especially to how referrals can be interpreted in order to understand something about the family and/or referrer. In essence this means formulating hypotheses about the family and family-referrer system, even though the therapists may have only a very brief referral and have not seen the family. For the present we would ask you to think of a hypothesis as just any story that would fit the known facts. Hypothesising is covered in great detail in Chapter 4, and all of the topics raised in this chapter are taken up in later chapters. For the purposes of getting going, you just need to take on the ideas at the basic level at which we introduce them in this chapter.

In order to form helpful hypotheses therapists need to construe the symptoms and difficult behaviours in a positive way. Positive connotations, discussed in Chapter 1, are one way of doing this. Usually one member in the family is the carrier of specific symptoms or behaviours which the rest of the family or extended systems such as school, work, and hospital, find difficult to deal with and understand. Thinking about the function of the behaviour in a positive sense may help to construct hypotheses which differ from the way the family have been thinking about themselves. This provides a foundation for the family for thinking about doing things differently.

Referral

Families everywhere go through times when they are under stress. Such periods can often be interpreted as a developmental stage or life cycle process where one or more family members have transitions to negotiate (Dare, 1979). When this occurs most families find solutions to their problems and move on having resolved the difficulties in their very own style. There is no such thing as a 'normal' family. Rather, families in most cases find ways of being, interacting and coping which make sense to them and allow individuals within the family system to develop more or less ordinarily. It is when a family gets 'stuck' or experiences 'going round in circles', when their solutions do not serve them well anymore, that a referral to family therapy is acceptable.

Referrals may come from a variety of sources: professionals, courts, one family member with or without everyone's knowledge, family sub-system, neighbours, member of the extended family. This very possibility requires practitioners to think systemically. Recognising the number of people or agencies that could be engaged, either singly or jointly, in making a referral or working with a family, requires consideration of who else is involved and how.

How to Respond to and Interpret the Referral

The way a referral is received and approached is itself a communication and intervention to the family. Seeking or being referred for help evokes emotions, behaviours and expectations which, if not recognised and elicited, may influence the family away from engaging in the work and frustrate the formation of a therapeutic alliance. The encounter is a co-evolving system involving anxieties, defences, transference and countertransference (Preston-Shoot and Agass, 1990). For example, if a family member's previous experiences of caring relationships or encounters with professionals has left negative feelings, these may seep into present relationships. Again, anxiety about seeking help may result in vagueness, flooding the therapist with information, or immediate demands for solutions. If therapists do not explore these dynamics, families may disengage, believing that their feelings are not respected. Equally, by setting the scene through explaining why contact is occurring and how the therapists work, and by conveying openness through exploring family members' ways of seeing the problem, family members are more likely to feel respected, their experiences acknowledged.

The circumstances, the person and the reason for making the referral in a specific way provide a great deal of information and usually say something about the family. It is helpful, therefore, to build hypotheses of the family and their difficulties, addressing key questions: what is the problem; what is the meaning or function of the problem; why has the referral come now; why worry? The information gathered at this stage should be centred around these questions.

If the referral comes from a professional and is written simply: 'I would be grateful for your opinion on this family', it may be reasonable to infer anything from severe problems to minor difficulties, and hypotheses will need to be wide ranging. It may also be prudent to get in touch with the referrer and request more detail. On the other hand a referral may be very detailed about the family. Two points are important when receiving a long referral: first, to extract relevant information, develop a chronological picture of events, and construct a geneogram; secondly, to distinguish between the opinions and hypotheses of the referrer about the family and their problem(s), and the factual information given regarding this family.

It is advisable at this early stage to enquire whether any other professionals are involved with the family and whether they know of the referral. There are no hard and fast rules about whether other professionals should be informed that a family is coming for therapy but good practice, a sense of freedom and flexibility suggest that this issue should be carefully considered alongside the nature of the referral and openly discussed with the referrer and family.

The second step is to inform the family that a referral has been received and to invite them for an assessment session. We do not request further information from the family but leave that task until we meet with them.

A telephone enquiry by the professional or family may result in a date and time for an assessment session. This invariably includes discussion both about the family therapy and the family. When speaking with either the professional referrer or the family referrer it is important to maintain a considerable degree of 'neutrality' (see Chapters 4 and 7), to avoid taking sides or becoming enmeshed.

Both family and referred may be given information about family therapy and working with families. We have found that if the referrer and family knew that family therapy was carried out by a team, and that with their permission the sessions would be filmed the family arrived in a different frame of mind. Referrers did not express their possible scepticism and influence the family in a negative way.

The Professionals' Meeting

Particularly if the family, or individual members of the family, have been receiving help from other agencies it may be necessary to have a professionals' meeting before making the first appointment with the family. When other professionals refer a family they have usually made considerable effort to effect some changes in the family system. When the thought of further help grows out of a feeling that both the family and professional have come to an impasse, family therapists must recognise that such a referral encompasses and must address not only the problem of the family but the agenda of the professional. The referring professional and family have in this sense joined to become one system. Therefore, consideration must be given to whether the professional system has become part of the problem rather than the solution.

Accordingly, it is important to hypothesise about the position of the referrer in the referred person's system if the therapists are not to become embroiled in the family-referrer system and, thereby, lose their influence and leverage (Selvini Palazzoli, Boscolo, Cecchin and Prata, 1980b). Analysing the dynamics around the referral process may uncover 'referral games' (Preston-Shoot and Agass, 1990). The referrer may feel anxious about or stuck in their role with a family. Alternatively, they may be avoiding challenging the family about particular issues. In seeking to refer the family, their objective may be to 'protect' or 'save' their position with the family. Focusing on the interactions between referrer and referred may help therapists to avoid being triangulated, sought as an ally by one party against another or by both to stabilise and 'save' their conflictual or unstable relationship (Carl and Jurkovic, 1983).

Thus, it is useful to consider such questions as: who is making this referral, for whom, and for what purpose? Why is the problem a problem? In which system does the problem lie? Who is the customer? Where are people in relation to each other? What changes do they and the family want? Are these the same or different? What is not being said or what is being denied and concealed on referral? By hypothesising, practitioners will arrive at an interactional formulation concerning the sequences which maintain behaviour in the referrer-family system and which have led to referral. This may indicate whether, in which system, and how to intervene.

The professionals' meeting has the function of bringing together all the professionals who may be involved in the family. In this meeting the boundaries between the professionals, their specific involvement, and role in the family needs to be ascertained. Most of all each professional must share their agenda, that is what they expect and hope the family therapists will achieve/undertake with the family. We have recognised over and over again what a destructive influence a disappointed professional can be in the work with the family. The family can easily be pulled in a number of directions because they cannot bear or afford to displease the professionals they see. Consequently, the professionals' meeting itself should be conducted with a maximum of awareness of the boundaries, duties and responsibilities everyone has.

Example of a Professionals' Meeting

The team, after receiving a referral from a social worker, telephoned and discussed the possibility of a professionals' meeting, the date and place of such a meeting and who else should be invited. The referring social worker explained that a probation officer was involved with one member of the family, that there was a very young baby and a health visitor visited the home regularly. There had been a particular problem with school attendance and an educational psychologist had visited the family and made some input at school with regard to one child's behaviour there. Though the grandmother of the family lived next door the family functioned as one and the grandmother would wish to attend the sessions. The grandmother had been under the care of a psychiatrist for a year because she had become distressed and anxious. The social worker felt that it would be important to invite the psychiatrist because he had indicated that if grandmother separated from the family she would feel better.

A date was fixed and a letter of invitation to the meeting was sent out to everyone. On the day the social worker, probation officer, general practitioner, health visitor and the family's psychiatrist attended.

The family therapy team had decided who would conduct the meeting and introduce their way of working to the meeting. This therapist/conductor, after asking everyone into the room opened with: "Welcome. Thank you for coming. My name is . . . I would like to suggest two things before we begin our discussion of the . . . family. I would like to explain to you briefly how we work here and then you can introduce yourselves.

Working with families is a complex business and most family therapists work in a team of at least two or more. This is the case here as well. We work in a team of six, including myself. The rest of the team are sitting behind this one-way mirror. Crudely speaking their job is to help the therapist help the family, or in the case of a meeting – the meeting. You are of course welcome to meet the team and the team would like to meet you. Once I have finished with my explanation they will come out. You have probably also noticed the cameras in the room and we would like to ask you to give permission to film this meeting. The cameras are not filming now and will only be switched on if you all agree.

The filming helps us to do two things: to keep an accurate record of the meeting and to look back on it to remind ourselves of what we have discussed and possibly agreed. The video of this meeting may also be looked at by you to refresh your memory. For families the process is similar: they may wish to look at certain aspects of a previous session and the team most certainly look at the video between sessions, both to check on the tasks but also to learn more about the family. Each time one looks at the video one discovers more detail which in the long term may be crucial in understanding the family and assisting change. We explain this in greater detail to the family than we are doing with you today. We also have the option to erase the video at the end of the session. This is particularly important if some or all members of the meeting feel that they do not wish to have this kind of record of the session. We ask to indicate this at the end of the session/meeting if you feel you do not wish a video to be kept. You may also have noticed that I am wearing an earpiece (or there is a telephone). This is so that the team can communicate brief messages to me, which I will usually pass on. When we see families I also leave the room for approximately ten minutes or sometimes a little longer to consult with the team towards the end of the session. We use this time to formulate our thoughts and ideas about the family into an intervention or message. A message and/or intervention* from the team will then be presented to the family, often including a task. This is not the format with this meeting today, but should the team have a longer message they will either ask me to come out and join them or they may send one member out and tell me/us what they have thought about. If I leave the room to join the team the video will be switched off and the blind pulled down so that you are not observed and have privacy. The family are also told this. We have decided to tell you all this in this way because that is how we conduct the sessions with the families too and we wanted you to be aware how this is done. We also explain that the video tape is strictly confidential and only available to the team and yourselves (the meeting or family). It can only be viewed in this clinic. Have you any questions just about this way of working? May I ask you whether you would agree to the filming?"

*(see Chapters 5 and 6)

When the questions about the 'way of working' have been discussed we proceed to the introductions.

If there are requests to see behind the screen and/or look at the video equipment this request is always granted whether in a family or professionals' meeting. In our experience, if these preliminaries are clear, most professionals and families feel involved and valued rather than suspicious.

Exercise 3.1 (15 minutes)
Role-play this introduction adapting it to your situation.

The professionals' meeting then discusses how family therapy might help the family and what each professional thinks the difficulties of the family are. The role of each professional must also be established and that family therapy will not replace them or their work.

Only when the professionals have agreed that the family should be invited for an assessment session and their thoughts elicited on how family therapy will help is an appointment arranged. If it transpires that some of the keyworkers are quite ambivalent or opposed to family therapy, a second professionals' meeting might have to be arranged.

Professionals' meetings can be called at any time. It is important to let the family know, and to make sure that they receive feedback. Except, possibly, in exceptional circumstances, there is no reason why the family could not take part if that is what they requested. Indeed, organisations like Family Service Units (Family Service Units, 1982) involve families as a matter of policy in referral and review meetings.

Key Worker Joining the Family for Therapy

Sometimes it becomes very clear during the professionals' meeting that the family would not attend without either the social worker or other significant figure present and this needs to be agreed. If a professional joins the family in the therapy sessions a professionals' meeting can be used to work out how precisely this is going to work. Is this worker part of the team, or part of the family? We have found that, in the sessions, the key worker who joins the family needs to be seen as part of the family system, included in any circular questions and interventions.

Indicators for Accepting or Not Accepting a Family for Therapy

In most cases referrals lead to an assessment session without professionals' meetings and it is at that stage that a decision is made whether to offer the family some therapy sessions. The family is encouraged to decide whether they wish to work in this way. It must be accepted that many families would not find it easy to make such a decision and in this case the therapy commences. It is not necessary that each member of the family attends the sessions though it does help if they can attend at least once. It is perfectly feasible to work with sub-systems and to include absent members through particular circular questions (see Chapter 4).

In our experience there are some indicators that we recognise for not accepting families before we have even seen them. They are as follows:

1) When there is clear evidence that a key professional involved in the care of the family or an individual member of the family is categorically opposed to the therapy.

2) When the task is to achieve a specific change in the system which is felt to be appropriate by other professionals but not the family.

3) Sometimes families are sent for therapy by a Court. If the family is totally against this and only attend because they have been sentenced in this way, the element of compulsion is likely to sabotage any effective work.

Inviting the Family for an Assessment Session

The assessment session is always arranged by letter even if the family has telephoned the clinic to receive further information or a professional has also passed on the appointment date and time. The main reason is that by writing the family have in their possession a letter which gives them the title and address of the venue they are coming to and it is signed by a person to whom they can refer either at the time or at a later date. A map and stamped addressed envelope, asking the family whether they can attend or not, is good practice.

In preparation for the session the team should form hypotheses, arrange for one member of the team to be the therapist, and one member to be what we call the 'secretary'. It is the 'secretary' who lets the family in and out of the building and who conducts the initial introductions to the family. In this way the 'therapist' remains free to carry out the therapy. However, we regard this as a way which works for us and offer it as a suggestion not as a rule.

Once the family is taken into the room where the therapy takes place the 'secretary' introduces the clinic and 'how we work' in a similar way to that described in the example above of the professionals' system. The family is encouraged to ask questions about 'how we work' and if questions about the problem or family arise the 'secretary' lets the family know that the therapist will discuss this with them. The 'secretary' then leaves and the 'therapist' enters. If the family have all indicated that they are prepared to have the session filmed, the video is then switched on. The introductions take place and the therapist repeats once more a request to film. This ensures that the consent is 'on record' and makes it unnecessary to sign consent forms. Again, this is only one method of dealing with this issue.

Since at our centre we also do research we inform the family of this fact. They are told who has access to the material and that confidentiality is strictly adhered to. If we have visitors or trainees we say so and will introduce them to the family. As with the professionals' meeting we also make clear to the family that they can request that the video is wiped after each session.

If the family wish to meet the team, or if they wish to view the room behind the screen they may do this now or at a later time. Many families are much more anxious to get on with what they have come about than to fit in with our anxieties and agendas. It is important to recognise this and follow the family rather than to impose our wishes unnecessarily.

Families sometimes object to the team behind the screen and if we have not been able to make it clear that this is in their interest as much as in our own, and that it does help then the team may agree to move into the room for that session.

A 'one-way mirror' is used in family therapy to allow the interaction between clients and therapists to be observed (Persaud, 1987). The mirror is used essentially as a 'device to look through', a relatively neutral piece of technology designed to intrude as little as possible in the immediate process of therapy (Cade and Cornwell, 1985). A one-way mirror can also be used to enhance supervision and training, providing a meta view of the therapist-family system (see Chapter 8).

The assessment meeting is so-called deliberately because a contract for therapy is not agreed until family members have had the opportunity to give informed consent on the basis of knowing what the therapists offer, and the therapists have had the opportunity of considering what they can offer after hearing how the family have 'arrived', how each member views the problems, and what changes they want and will settle for.

Forming the Initial Hypotheses

In preparation for the assessment session hypotheses should be formulated from the referral information. A hypothesis is a story that could account for the information available. There is a difference between a systemic hypothesis (see Chapter 4) and a working hypothesis. It is the latter that we will briefly describe here.

A hypothesis opens up some interesting questions about the family system. At the stage of referral it directs practitioners to thinking about 'what problem was the symptom trying to solve', 'what solutions have been attempted', 'in what way was it successful', and 'why is it not successful now', 'why have the family sought help and at this moment in time'. Depending on the information a number of hypotheses can be generated even when there is very little material available. Forming hypotheses is not something new, we all do it much of the time. It is a way to organise information more clearly. All of us have ideas and thoughts about any new family we are about to encounter. Formally thinking about these ideas brings them into the open and spells them out. This provides therapists with a basis to follow a line of enquiry and test it out.

Exercise 3.2(30 minutes)

Formulating hypotheses
A referral letter has been received from a consultant paediatrician. You are preparing to see the family. Write down the hypotheses you have formulated using the letter and any other information you might have.

> Dear . . .
>
> *Re: Steptoe family.*
>
> You may remember that your agency has worked with this family periodically for a number of years. Each of the children in turn has presented with difficulties: truancy, enuresis, general unhappiness and under-functioning, especially at school. The situation now is that the oldest child, Albert (24), has left home. Peter (18) and Marion (17) still live at home. Peter works but Marion is expecting a child and hopes to leave home shortly. The parents, Ron and Freda, have had a difficult, unhappy marriage.
>
> The present problem centres around the youngest child, Rachel (12) whose school attendance has led to court appearances and the possibility of her reception into care. Both Rachel and her parents are exceedingly worried about this threat. In addition, Rachel seems an unhappy child. She is under-functioning at school. She talks about arguments between her parents about money and the condition of the house which, I understand, is full of rubbish.
>
> I would be grateful for your help.
>
> Yours sincerely,

1) Formulate as many hypotheses as you can, but at least three.

2) Organise your hypotheses into topics if this seems useful. Be creative and imagine what this family might be like, thereby developing hypotheses which relate as much to your belief system about families as to the family. It is important to bring into the open and discuss what is in your head about the family and referral. This can be of immense help. It is increasingly recognised that, if practitioners are not to become emotionally overloaded by or embroiled in the complexity of working with families and the disturbing, powerful emotional forces which can be encountered, they must comprehend their reactions to

material and examine their own unresolved or hidden feelings. Self-awareness is crucial if therapists are to remain open, reflective and responsive. Thus, in relation to this case, for instance, what does the material trigger in you? Are there any parallels with your own family experience which this case might reactivate? What does the prospect of working with this family evoke in you?

Constructing a Geneogram

A geneogram is an elaborate form of family tree, a visual conceptualisation of a family or other system: its structure, relationships, bonds. It may encompass several generations or hierarchies and incorporate age; gender; race; class; life events such as birth, marriage, divorce, and death; health; family roles. It has become an important tool when considering referrals and when working with families. In part this is because it makes complex information more accessible (Heinl, 1985) and elicits themes, beliefs, patterns, rituals, 'secrets', and myths, and how these are transmitted across generations and have influenced family development. The process is basically one of using symbols (see Table 3.1) to represent people and their connectedness or inter-relationships.

Geneograms have several uses. First, as a way of taking a family history and drawing together information about family structure. When hypothesising about a referral and preparing for an assessment session, it helps therapists to organise the information they have about the family. It reveals gaps in knowledge and may suggest areas to explore. It helps therapists to hypothesise about what the problem is, why it is a problem now, and what the problem may be for.

Secondly, as a way of conveying information between family members and thereby introducing difference into the system. Thirdly, as a way of enabling the family to depict and understand family structure and dynamics. This use, as a therapeutic intervention, aims to enable family members to move towards different ways of interacting on the basis of awareness and recognition of emotionally charged material, and patterns that have influenced and constrained family behaviour: in other words, to free present choices from past influences (Lieberman, 1979).

In Chapter 7 we will discuss the latter two uses and how, interactively with family members, therapists may make visually explicit the family's structure and roles, denote boundaries, and indicate the nature of their emotional relationships (Lieberman, 1979). Here the focus is on the first use, with therapists compiling a geneogram from the available information as an aid to hypothesising and determining an initial focus of intervention.

Symbol meaning	Symbol
Male.	□
Female.	○
Gender unknown (e.g. pregnancy).	△
Permanent bond.	———
Short-term or transitory relationship	- - - -
Stressful.	/\/\/\/\/\/\
Strong bond.	═══
Weak bond/distance.	....
Miscarriage or abortion.	
Adopted.	or A
Fostered.	F
Deceased.	⊠ or ⊗
Temporarily Separated.	
Separated.	
Divorced.	

Table 3.1 Symbols for a geneogram

Exercise 3.3 (30 minutes)

Building a geneogram
Take the Steptoe family as an example, using the symbols shown in the table. Begin with Mr and Mrs Steptoe

FREDA RON

We know that they have children: Albert

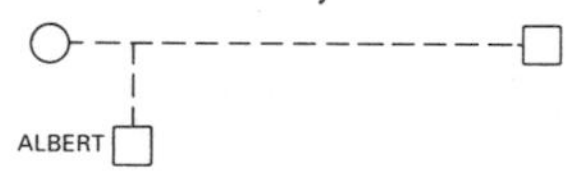

Peter

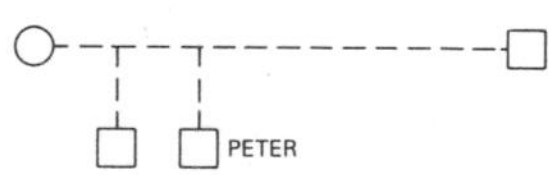

Marion, whom we know to be pregnant

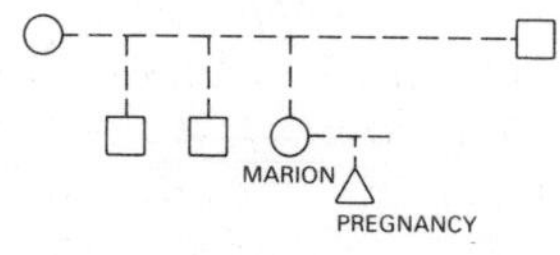

and we know that the youngest child in the family, called Rachel, is the focus of concern this time

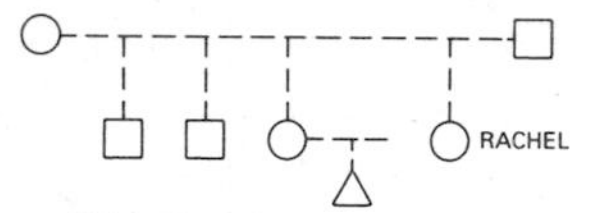

Completed in stages, a geneogram of the family, as known at referral, now exists. Now, reconsider the hypotheses obtained earlier from the referral letter.

Exercise 3.4 (45 minutes)

Constructing a personal geneogram
In pairs, each construct a personal family geneogram. At this stage, just elicit who is in the family, as we have done with the Steptoe family. Keep the geneogram and in Chapter 7 we will focus on the process by which you did this task, what this might say, and the nature of relationships in your family. Once again, the rationale for this personal work is the importance of identifying feelings, issues, patterns, and experiences in your own family, contemporary and past, which may be triggered by work with families.

Chapter 4

Hypothesising and Circular Questioning – Defining the Problem

In family therapy the crucial task is to develop an understanding of how the family has come to be stuck. More accurately, the task is to construct a story that will enable the therapists to do something that will enable the family to move in a direction of its choice. This story does not pretend to be a definitive and comprehensive account and so we call it an *Hypothesis* to indicate that it is tentative, up for testing, and open to continual modification or disproof. Chapter 3 discussed the pre-session therapist – team meeting at which information is reviewed, hypotheses formulated or revised, and routes for questioning devised. Chapter 5 will address the formulation and delivery of interventions. In between, the therapist by means of circular questioning attempts to formulate and test out hypotheses, to elaborate the problem.

Hypothesising

Hypotheses co-evolve in the interactions between family, therapist and team. Built from the information available together with practice wisdom and a knowledge of theory, such as the life-cycle transitions which families must negotiate, hypotheses are metaphors or conjectures. That is, they are are not so much truths as more or less useful formulations (Selvini Palazzoli, Boscolo, Cecchin and Prata, 1980a), validated, modified or abandoned during circular questioning. To get away from the worry of 'is it really true' let us think of an hypothesis as a story (one of many possible) that therapists tell each other about the family as a source of ideas about how things could be different. Now for hypotheses to help, they cannot just be any old story. For example, 'If they won a million on the pools; there is no hope so long as grandmother has such power; if only they would all try a bit harder; they are doing it to spite me.' These are all common kinds of story that offer no ideas about what might usefully be done to free the family.

Exercise 4.1 (15 minutes)
As a group, think of what you know about the Calderdales. Go round the circle with each person offering a dead-end hypothesis like the ones above, that is guaranteed to be of no help at all to a therapist. People who cannot think of that kind of hypothesis quickly enough should offer instead a platitude that would fit the circumstances of the family.

Usually we are surprised how easily and naturally we can think of unhelpful hypotheses.

A good hypothesis will give you a perspective that goes beyond that of the family, and gives a chance of 'leverage' – a way of identifying one of those points where a small amount of effort will bring about a large effect. Obviously stories like that are a good thing and they don't grown on trees. After all, if they were obvious they would be obvious to the family who have thought far more about their problem than we ever will. So this kind of hypothesis is inevitably a bit obscure and we will have to ask you to work with us while we list their characteristics and then show exactly what we mean. Meanwhile, we must point out that we are not asking you to give up what you already know about assessing families. Wilkinson (1987) shows how all forms of information about families are needed for a reliable account. Systemic hypothesising is about putting everything we can discover into its most useful form.

Hypotheses must be systemic: they must preserve therapist neutrality – challenging everyone or everything whilst aligning with no-one; they must positively connote each person's contribution to the system; they must include all the elements of the system and address the total relational function (Selvini Palazzoli, Boscolo, Cecchin and Prata, 1980a), that is, be about relationships expressed as circles or spirals; they must be expressed in terms of what people do and believe rather than what people 'are'. Thus, not 'Ron is aggressive and violent so he becomes angry whenever Freda does not have his meal ready.' This is a dead-end kind of comment open both to misinterpretation arising from its vagueness, and to the stuckness of a linear punctuation involving blame and the ascription of fixed immutable qualities. Rather, 'what you have described to us is that Ron looks angry when Freda does not have his meal ready and then . . . .' This enables therapist and family to track and clarify relationships without connoting the system as unchangeable or restricting therapist manoeuvrability.

One component suggested by Selvini Palazzoli, Boscolo, Cecchin and Prata (1980a), and that we have found essential to avoid just such a negative connotation, is the avoidance of the verb 'to be'. Instead, we talk of what is done, what is shown, what we see. Not Ron is angry but Ron looks angry; not Johnny is stupid but Johnny does stupid things; not Freda is emotional but Freda lets her emotions show; not Fred is frightened of . . . but Fred indicates that he thinks . . . is dangerous; not Mary is easily annoyed but Mary gives us an impression that she may show annoyance easily. The point of doing this is to invite enquiry, elaboration and detailed behavioural description by avoiding turning experience into stone. It is to move away from ascribing fixed qualities or characteristics to individuals, as if such things existed in their own right, because to describe someone as violent or aggressive, for instance, is of limited value because it addresses only one perspective on a system and masks the fact that meaning is given to behaviour on the basis of the context in which it occurs. If X and Y are arguing and then X hits Y, we may readily think that X is aggressive. But suppose Y is a child and X his mother, or we learn that Y was choking on a piece of food and the blow rescued her, or that X and Y are actors.

It is not just that we need to know the relationship in order to judge whether X was being aggressive, but that once we have a description of the behaviour and of the relationship, we have all we need in order to understand what will happen next. So an essential aspect of any hypothesis is to consider how individuals relate to each other; how they fit together; how they communicate, to whom, and what for (cf. Watzlawick, Beavin and Jackson, 1967; Selvini Palazzoli, Boscolo, Cecchin and Prata, 1978; Tomm, 1984). Because we are, with families, mostly concerned about relationships, it is almost always essential for the hypothesis not only to include an account of the relationships, but to see the symptom, the problem, and other behaviour in terms of the effect they have on relationships. A problematic behaviour may have developed in order to hold certain people together, or keep them apart; to force a relationship on people; or to prevent a relationship from changing. So a question that arises very early in developing hypotheses is 'how has the symptom affected relationships within the family'.

Exercise 4.2 (30 minutes)
Sit in pairs, preferably with a colleague or someone you know. In turns, the first person should state one of their characteristics in the form 'I am . . .'. The second person is to convert that statement into a description of behaviour, belief, or presentation, as in the examples above. Do this for five examples each. Then discuss whether the alternative description allowed you to feel any greater choice or control over the tendencies you chose to present.

With many of the techniques we are introducing, the exercises just give a preliminary indication or break the ice, so that you can see that it would be possible to operate in this way. We then rely on you to take them away and practise them in work settings. We have found that it is very useful to have a phase of exaggerating the techniques for a while until they become habitual. You may find it is possible to have quite a lot of fun doing this, especially if you can practise with a partner or group.

One key skill in hypothesising is to maintain openness, characterised by avoidance of preconceptions, labels and stereotypes, and a search based on curiosity for different meanings and ways of understanding how family or system members interact, how their behaviour and structure fit together. As many different possibilities should be produced to enable circular or spiralling patterns to be seen and circular questions to be asked (Cecchin, 1987). This openness includes, importantly, having regard for the not so obvious since what is critical may not be easily or immediately observable. It involves, therefore, not rushing in with a favourite hypothesis, or with solutions or interpretations but, by applying a meta perspective or internal supervisor (Casement, 1985), approaching the material with a concerned curiosity or playfulness and a considered use of practice experience and theoretical underpinnings.

Closure, on the other hand, would be imposing one hypothesis by responding to theory and prejudice rather than the material. There is no one answer and therapists who pursue it are likely to appear distant, rehearsed, unreal and intrusive. Accordingly, therapists should conduct a self-scrutiny: 'What do I not want to hear or see? What do I want to hear?' Equally, even if one hypothesis appears to fit, others should be explored. In that sense, hypotheses may be compared to trial identifications and interpretations in psychodynamic psychotherapy (Casement, 1985). What experience is being described? What does it feel like to be this individual in this family, in relation to this person? Hypotheses co-evolve. Not truths, their utility derives from the extent to which they enable system members to understand and unravel the difficulties which oppress them. They mark the beginnings of enquiry.

The basic requirements of a systemic hypothesis are summarised in Table 4.1. Having this list makes it easier to check whether any important feature has been overlooked. We therefore suggest that you use the Table to check any hypotheses that you create or encounter from now on. However, we are not suggesting that hypotheses are no use unless they meet all of these criteria. But knowing just where the hypothesis is and is not fully systemic helps us to understand how it works.

Exercise 4.3 (30 minutes)
Separate into groups of four and construct a hypothesis concerning Jill Calderdale getting into trouble. You are likely to have to start with a fairly linear punctuation, but try to focus this first idea on the effects of the problem on all of the relationships within the family. Simultaneously you should ensure that you consistently positively connote, remain neutral, and avoid the verb 'to be' by converting nouns and

verbs (he is depressive, he is depressed) into adjectives or adverbs (he behaves in a depressed way by . . .). As you generate a series of linear hypotheses, try to build them into a story of a circular or even better a spiral process. As you get near the end refer to Table 4.1 to check your hypothesis meets all of the requirements.

Then, the whole group should reconvene, and each group of four present its hypothesis.

The group should discuss how the different hypotheses can be seen as alternative stories that can be put alongside each other, and how far they might be combined into a single, more general, hypothesis.

Finally, check the general hypothesis against Table 4.1 and make any changes needed to fit all seven points.

---

*Once you have an hypothesis you will want to do something with it, but as we said earlier, constructing systemic hypotheses is the core skill of systemic family therapy and is quite difficult. We therefore want to continue our exploration before proceeding in the next chapter to use them.

Table 4.1

	Characteristics of a systemic hypothesis
1	Is circular
2	Is about relationships
3	Is expressed in terms of what people do and believe, rather than what they are
4	Preserves therapist neutrality
5	Includes all members of the family system
6	Positively connotes everyone
7	Is meta to the family's hypothesis

Why Hypothesise?

Hypotheses serve three purposes. For therapist and team, hypotheses provide organisation and illumination: that is, frameworks for direction and travel in exploration; boundaries to ensure structured, focused and disciplined enquiry; understanding and meaning as a basis for tracing, clarifying and modifying relationship patterns and sequences. Hypotheses provide a holding function. They enable therapist and team to stay meta, even under extreme pressure, rather than be sucked down and into a family script or dynamic, and to avoid muddled, mindless-doing characterised by being overwhelmed by the material, drift or purposeless activity. Once found to be useful they suggest actions to promote and obtain change.

Secondly, hypotheses provide a good guide to progress. If unable to develop hypotheses, therapist and team may have either become infatuated with one idea and/or accepted and become enmeshed in the family's punctuation, thereby losing leverage and manoeuvrability and becoming stuck (Cecchin, 1987). Thirdly, for family or system members, hypotheses are one means of introducing new information, thereby opening up the system to other than the linear punctuations in which they are entrapped.

Forming Hypotheses

It is helpful to begin hypotheses with 'in this family . . .' or 'in this system . . .' and then frame them by considering what might be going on that illuminates what people are doing and how they perceive relationships in the system. There are, in essence, three questions. The first, *who for*, reflects on the reason for referral and the role of the referring person. This was analyzed in Chapter 3. The second question, *what for*, addresses the need to hypothesise about the problem referred. What is it? Who is it (most) a problem for? What maintains the problem and what does it attempt to solve, prevent or trigger? Formulations should be as simple as possible. These fundamental questions address relationships, actions and interactions. Thus, therapist and team should hypothesise about where the problem resides: between people, between people and other systems, or between systems (Specht and Vickery, 1977); what assumptions, scripts or myths, historical or socially constructed within society, such as gender roles, influence the functioning of the system; what solutions have been attempted, in what way all the solutions tried are of the same type and why they could not be abandoned.

The third question, *why now*, points to those changes, perhaps approaching life cycle transitions or events outside the system, which demand differences to relationships and which are resisted because of the challenges this poses. The three questions are basic ingredients to forming hypotheses and to, therefore, the interventions which are inspired by them.

Exercise 4.4 (1 hour)

To generate systemic hypotheses, we suggest a three stage process using the case material here to test its feasibility.

First, in groups of four, consider the referral information. The Steptoe family comprises:

1) father, Ron, skilled labourer, aged 50
2) mother, Freda, housewife, aged 48
3) son, Albert, in the navy, aged 24
4) son Peter, baker, aged 18
5) daughter, Marion, unemployed, aged 17
6) daughter, Rachel, at school, aged 12

All the family live at home except Albert who returns occasionally on leave but then usually stays with his wife's family. Peter and Marion spend considerable periods of time out of the house, including staying overnight with friends. Marion is planning to marry a friend of Albert's in the next few months. All the children appear closest to Freda, with the possible exception of Rachel who appears close to both her parents.

The presented 'problem' is Rachel whose school attendance has now been referred to the Juvenile Court. The Magistrates are considering making a care order. This has provoked considerable anxiety, distress and anger in the family, especially for Freda and Rachel. When they poured this out to a paediatrician, who was seeing Rachel for a follow-up appointment following treatment after being knocked down by a car several years ago, she referred the case to your agency.

The family have been known to your agency for over ten years. All the children have under-achieved at school and truanted. The house, on a local 'sink' estate, is in poor condition. It is described as a 'mess' and a 'tip', with years of accumulated rubbish and possessions cluttering up every room. Workmen have refused to do repairs in the house and health inspectors have been called to the house by neighbours on several occasions. The family cannot sit together in any of the rooms. There is only a narrow passage way through each room between the rubbish. None of the doors can open fully.

There have been long-standing marital difficulties. Ron is known to drink very heavily, to keep the family short of money, such that Freda is always in debt. Ron is angry that Freda does voluntary work at the local community centre most days and evenings of the week. He also complains about lack of sex. Freda is described by everyone as depressed. All the family define it as her job to clean the house but she feels too depressed to do so. She complains that none of the children help her. She has tried several times to leave Ron but has always returned.

The family have been told that they are unhelpable and they feel themselves to be so. Previous family work has been along the lines of a task-centred model, usually at times of crisis when the Juvenile Court has been threatening action about the children's schooling. Tasks have been set about ensuring school attendance and clearing the house of 'mess.' This has worked for short periods, the case has been closed, and the 'mess' and truancy has returned.

Now, in your groups of four, generate as many conjectures as possible. These may be either linear or circular, ranging from the highly probable to the quite unlikely. They may be based on the material in conjunction with theoretical understanding, practice wisdom, curiosity and/or intuition. At this stage we are not after complete hypotheses, but ideas that can subsequently be put together.

Some examples of partial hypotheses could be that in this family Ron seems angry to which Freda responds by withdrawing (no sex, depression) at which Ron complains and Freda withdraws further. Or, in this system Ron and Freda are aware of but stuck in conflicts. There is a rule not to discuss them because of the stuckness but the tension increases. Rachel plays a role to deflect the tension and focus away from Freda and Ron. This triangulation, however, distracts but does not solve, and still leaves them aware of and stuck in conflicts.

Next, connect the hypotheses into one or more circular hypotheses and check each of them against Table 4.1. The first thing to be done with an hypothesis is to test it. Every well formulated hypothesis will throw up interesting questions which will either test the idea or enrich it. Once the hypotheses have been stated, use them to consider the areas which suggest themselves for questioning.

Thus, first, this family system is in transition. The older children have left or are leaving. Rachel is the last. She is being 'held' by the ailing marriage. Other children are, therefore, 'released' from duty. Questions here may focus on how other 'departures' have been managed. The older children could be asked to comment. Questions about the future may be useful: 'when Rachel does grow up and leave, what will Ron and Freda do?' etc.

Secondly, Rachel is 'triangulated' in the marriage. Conflict is detoured through her. Questions here may focus on who would be most/least affected by her removal from home; who will miss her most etc. Rachel's behaviour can be positively connoted as bringing in outside help, and the questioning may bring parental conflict more into the open, thereby letting Rachel off the hook.

Thirdly, the 'mess' is a distance regulator. The family is 'disengaged': rooms are so rubbishy that family members cannot sit down together. There are few 'connecting doors' between them. Fresh information is blocked from circulating in the system. Questions here may explore 'differences' around the mess, perhaps positively connoting it as a means of helping children to leave, encouraging family members to go out and develop outside interests, and preventing too many heated scenes if they spent too much time in each other's company.

The exercise can be repeated, as it is in therapy, once questioning has elicited more information, the hypotheses being reviewed, modified, retained or abandoned. In the Steptoe family, further questioning elicited considerable information, given here as roles.

Exercise 4.5 (40 minutes)
Form into groups of seven or more. Five of the group are to role-play the Steptoe family, while the rest are to be therapists or, at this stage, hypothesis explorers. If your groups need to be nine or more, Albert can be home on leave, so six people will play the family.

The family should go off with the role descriptions given at the end of this chapter. Each person is to read their own role, then the family should discuss the problem of the mess at home in the most realistic way possible, until called in by the therapists.

While the family are getting into role, the therapists should take the hypothesis from the last exercise and write down a series of questions to test and explore it. You may wish to modify the hypothesis to put it in a form that makes exploration easier. Spend 10 minutes on this, then decide which two should be therapists to ask the questions while the others observe. Now collect your family, invite them to introduce themselves, and proceed with the questioning.

Question for 15 minutes. At the end of that time, the 'family' should de-role in a ritual way as described in the Introduction. Now reconsider your hypothesis in the light of the questioning. Has it been contradicted? Does any part need modifying or extending?

If you managed to stay close to your hypothesis you will have found it quite easy to stick to a productive line of questioning. Milan systemic family therapy has developed its own unique methods of questioning which are especially effective in generating the kind of information needed to test and enrich systemic hypotheses. In order to illustrate these methods, we offer one of the several hypotheses that one could construct about the Steptoe family. It fulfils the requirements for a systemic hypothesis. It is meta to the family's hypothesis: that something is wrong with Rachel or Freda (because she will not have sex) or Ron (because he is angry). It includes everyone and is circular, expressed in terms of interactions and relationships. 'Why now' appears answered by Rachel's leaving possibly being brought forward by the Juvenile Court, creating anxiety about what will happen next. The family therefore, seek to recruit a therapist to 'change' Rachel but not the family, in order to maintain their solution. The hypothesis maintains neutrality and leverage: it does not matter where therapy begins. The system cannot remain the same.

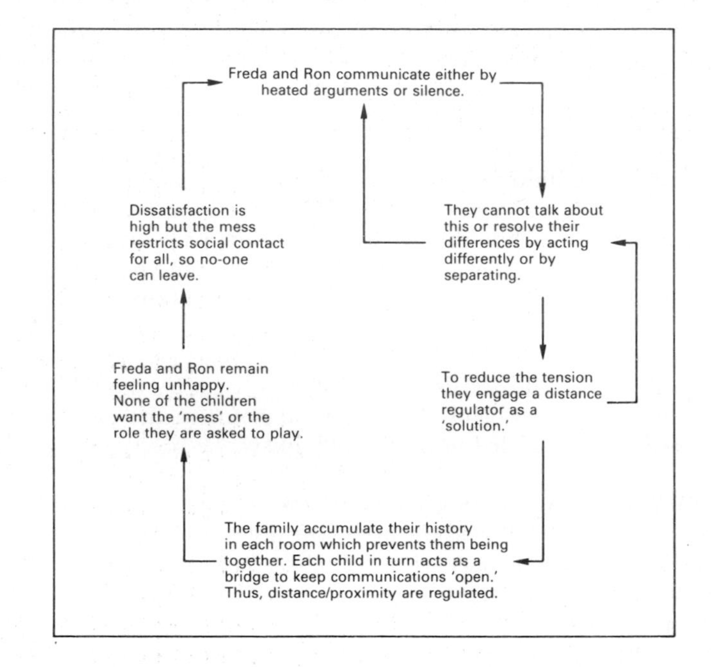

Figure 4.1

This hypothesis demonstrates some key principles in family dynamics. First, a third person (in this case Rachel) may become triangulated to enable two others to detour and avoid their conflict. If the third person moves too close to either member of the dyad, the other is threatened. If the third person seeks to leave the field, anxiety about what will happen next will increase and efforts will be made to retain the individual's 'services.'

Secondly, some families become trapped in a too far – too close system. Thus, for instance, when Freda has fears about intimacy with or separation from Ron, a symptomatic third person is engaged to stabilise the situation. When Freda's fears about separation increase, Rachel's problems bring Ron and Freda closer. When intimacy threatens, Rachel's behaviour will distract them (Byng-Hall and Campbell, 1981).

Thirdly, symptoms may be a mechanism for regulation, the family being a self-regulatory system (Papp, 1980). Thus, therapists will encounter resistance to change because the symptom regulates the dysfunctional part of the system. If 'cured', the system will feel unstable, unregulated.

Finally the stability of the system depends on there being constraints which prevent the symptom from getting out of hand, or the system breaking up. The mess as a solution is stable as it produces external regulators – because of the mess the family members tend to be unacceptable outside, so the children are picked on at school and stay home. Freda and Ron can't bring in friends who might disturb the balance but because of what is known about the state of their home, are unattractive to possible alternative permanent partners.

Hypothesis Testing: Circular Questioning

Hypotheses are rarely static. New information introduced into one part of the system will cause change to reverberate throughout the entire system. There is nothing so permanent as change. Systems are like moving sculpts. Inject energy into one area and the sculpt cannot remain unmoved. This movement is created by circular questioning.

Why circular? Information comes from difference (Bateson, 1973). In practice, this implies that practitioners learn more about phenomena by approaching them from various, different angles. Systems are not infrequently locked in battles over linear punctuations. Circular questioning is extremely effective at unlocking this stuckness and illuminating the interconnectedness of the system's parts. This is because the respondent is placed in a meta position, beyond the system in which they are usually enmeshed (Selvini Palazzoli, Boscolo, Cecchin and Prata, 1980a; O'Brian and Bruggen, 1985), able to observe and comment on transactional processes. This cuts across resistance to change because the respondent cannot not communicate, and yet is not directly commenting about themselves or their relationships. A is not asked about A or about AB so much as about B and others. This addresses and opens up relationships: actions, perceptions, beliefs, behaviour and feelings. It introduces new information by eliciting different perspectives on phenomena. Thus, who does Rachel feel afraid of? When Rachel feels afraid, what does she do? What happens then? Who helps Rachel feel less afraid? What do you think that person feels about Rachel's fear? As individuals cannot avoid describing relationships in answers (Penn, 1982) the circularity of the system, patterns and their connectedness, become apparent in stark contrast to the system's previous linear conceptualisations. Note that the first instruction of Exercise 2.1 used a circular question to help you perceive your own behaviour.

Involving each member in turn, avoiding questions which invite yes/no responses, and checking back with each how they see something on which others have commented, introduces feedback, maintains therapist neutrality, reduces the risk of being sucked into the system's script (Byng-Hall, 1988), elicits patterns and reveals differences in perceptions and punctuations. Indeed, it reveals how much members communicate and know about each other's feelings and thoughts.

Moreover, how the family reacts to this process is itself information, to integrate into hypotheses, about their response to the worker's hypotheses, how members communicate, how open or difficult their communication is, and whether verbal and non-verbal communication is congruent or divergent.

Circular questioning attempts to induce in the family an attitude of curiosity rather than defeat. The family will want to recruit you by X telling you how they have to live in terms that invite you to respond 'how awful!'. Then they have got you – you have joined them in their perception and are obliged to try to make 'it' better. Circular questioning keeps you out of this trap – it opens up the idea of alternative perspectives and lets you 'play' (though not in a disrespectful or disparaging way).

The different types of circular questions have been variously described (Selvini Palazzoli, Boscolo, Cecchin and Prata, 1980a; Hoffman, 1981; Penn, 1982; O'Brian and Bruggen, 1985; Burnham and Harris, 1988).

1) *Patterns of relationship and interactions*: when Ron complains to Freda about the state of the house, what does Rachel do? When Marion tells Freda she is going out, what does Ron say? What does Ron do when Freda says she is depressed? What happens when Rachel does not go to school?

2) *Hypothetical*: (i) informed 'guesses.' What do you think might happen to Ron and Freda if Rachel was taken into care? How would it be different? What would happen if Freda cleared the house? If Ron and Freda did not have to worry about Rachel's truancy, what would be a problem for them?

   (ii) using silence or absence. If Rachel were able to say what worries her most about Ron and Freda, what do you think she would say? If Albert were here, what might he say about how he experiences Ron and Freda's marriage?

   (iii) future oriented questions. Since anything can happen, what do you think Freda would like to be doing in five years' time? How might this family be different next year? If you look back in five years' time, how do you think you would describe this situation?

3) *Comparisons before and after*: since Marion has been at home, not working, has Rachel's school attendance been different? When did Rachel's truancy begin to be a problem? What else was happening then?

4) *Ranking to explore difference*: when Ron and Freda are not talking to each other, who gets most upset, who next . . .? Who is most worried about Rachel going into care, who next . . . (never 'who

least' if it would imply a negative connotation). Who is most concerned when Ron angrily shouts at Freda, who next? How do they show their concern?

5) *Historical*: when did this begin? What do you think is the most important/saddest/happiest event to have occurred in your family up to now? What did Ron/Freda do then? What changed, how were things different? How is this family the same as/different from your family when you were a child?

6) *Defining key, cue words*: when Freda says she is depressed, what does she do, how do you know? You say things have changed, what precisely is different? You say Rachel not going to school is a problem, how is that a problem for you? You say you have tried everything, what have you done? What happened? The objective is to define key words in terms of behaviour and relationships since therapists can be more helpful when meanings and situations are clarified. Defining words behaviourally opens out the possibility of change: what needs to be different, what can you or Ron do to enable you to feel less worried about Rachel? Vagueness provokes more of the same behaviour because it seems so large and amorphous, beyond control.

Exercise 4.6 (1 hour)

Hypothesis testing: circular questioning
In groups of four, ask as many circular questions as possible to establish what group members feel, think and know about family therapy, training, positive connotation, hypothesising, and their profession.

---

*In the same groups as the previous role-play, reconstitute the Steptoe family. While the family go off to get into role, the therapists should jot down a few circular questions to explore the hypothesis given in *Figure 4.1*. Now collect the family, say that you appreciate their having all come back for a second session, and proceed with your circular questioning. Observers may interrupt the session to feed circular questions to the therapists. If necessary, the therapists and observers could take a break to collect their thoughts, remind themselves of the hypothesis, and set up more circular questions. Allow twenty minutes for the role-play.

*At the end of the role-play, each family member should be asked by the therapist, to describe the experience of being circularly questioned. Now de-role, and discuss the experience, and any reformulation that the hypothesis now seems to need.

*As a final exercise from the role-play, consider how this practice avoids the family's linear views or individual punctuations and explores relationships, their understanding of each other's viewpoints, and communication patterns.

On past experience you are likely to have had two experiences during this exercise. First, that it is very difficult to remember the hypothesis and to consistently be circular in your questioning. Since people are used to asking direct questions, one useful technique is to consider what you would ask Freda, for example, then turn your face to ask the question to the person next to her, say Ron.

A second difficulty is likely to have arisen in keeping the role-play going because circular questions get very quickly to areas where information is lacking. If this happened, then the 'family' will have found that they had rapidly to invent information to be able to respond to the questions. In our view this is an indication of the power of circular questioning and it does suggest a possibility that role-plays only work when the questioning techniques are working rather superficially.

Hypothesis Testing: 'What is the Problem?'

One specific use to which circular questions can be put is to define the problem. Thus:

1) What is the problem? What do you think Rachel will say is the problem? Who agrees with Rachel? Who disagrees? How would you put it?
2) In what way is this problem a problem? What makes the problem a problem? How is it a problem for you?
3) Who is it most a problem for? Who next . . .?
4) Why now?

Therapists need two skills especially here. First, to pursue questioning to obtain specificity: 'Yes, but what is the problem?' Secondly, to be 'one down' to achieve this clarity: 'Maybe I'm not thinking clearly enough to understand you, but what makes this a problem for you now?'

A 'what is the problem' sequence is useful when either the family, family plus worker, or therapist and team have become stuck, locked in their attempted solutions or unable to identify hypotheses upon which to base one. This may occur for a variety of reasons and hypothesising about these may help to frame the actual questions. People may be reacting to what are ordinary life events or developments (Coulshed and Abdullah-Zadeh, 1985). There may be a fear of catastrophe: something is avoided, perhaps conflict or difference in a relationship. Alternatively, individuals (family member, therapist, referrer) may be recruited into the service of the family, the 'symptomatic' individual gaining something from this involvement. The system may not have any mechanism for reviewing and changing its organisation, its rules.

Finally, there may be disagreement regarding what the problem is or what should be done about it.

Therapists become stuck when, having been trained to think diagnostically and to think solutions, they slip into a favourite hypothesis or into prescriptions generated by the apparent familiarity of the problem. Another source of therapist stuckness, usually indicated by difficulty in generating hypotheses, is when workers are recruited into the system's problem definition, by the family and/or referrer. Thus, it is helpful to consider:

1) Where the problem is, in which system: between family members, between them and other systems, or between systems (Specht and Vickery, 1977). What part do various systems play in the problem?
2) Who identifies and refers the problem as a problem? What does this suggest about their position and about relationships in the system?
3) How problems are defined. What does this suggest about the referrer and the system?
4) Who may see themselves as 'losers' in the system. Where may resistance to change come from? How could this be positively connoted?
5) What change people want. What will happen if you do not enable this (Reder, 1986)? So, who most wants (what) change? What change do people want? What will they settle for (Lask, 1980)?

Therapists may feel 'press-ganged' into taking on a particular view, either from within themselves or from external pressures. The 'what is the problem?' sequence will enable workers to stand back and unravel processes.

Exercise 4.7 (20 minutes)

What is the problem?
In pairs, each construct an imaginary problem or identify an actual, personal issue. Spend 10 minutes one questioning the other. Find as many different circular ways of asking and clarifying 'what is the problem?'

Now analyse the process: how easy was it to avoid discussing solutions? How many solutions were considered? How effectively was the problem uncovered and understood? Does the questioner know who it is a problem for; how the respondent's mother/spouse/supervisor views it?

---

*A similar exercise consists of finding different ways to ask about and define the problem, taking each member of the Steptoe family in turn and asking both what they think others might say about the problem or about changes wanted, and about how they define the situation. What specificity in terms of behaviours and beliefs can you elicit?

Session 'Trips'

Change is frightening because it involves reaching for difference. Change is, therefore, not always readily welcomed and therapists may not be greeted with enthusiasm. Alternatively, initial keenness may soon turn into attempts at disqualification or sabotage (Selvini Palazzoli, Boscolo, Cecchin and Prata, 1980b, describe some fairly spectacular examples). It is, therefore, useful to consider how members of a system may try to trip up therapists, to anticipate 'what if?' questions and practise responses which maintain neutrality and manoeuvrability, stay meta and introduce difference. For example:

1) What if the Steptoe family sit passively, *waiting* for the therapist to say something?
2) What if Ron and/or Freda *ask if it is normal* for children to truant? What if they ask you *to tell them* why Rachel truants?
3) What if the family say they have tried everything and you, *as the expert*, must know what they should do? They ask for your opinion.
4) What if the family *seek reassurance* from you that something (feared but not always revealed as such) will not happen?

The phrases in italics represent common attempts to trip therapists. Practising responses is useful, such as 'who can say? What do you think?' to the question 'what is normal.' Here again, a circular orientation is invaluable. When confronted by a question that asks you to commit yourself in a way that may work against you in future, be circular. Turn to someone else and ask: what do you think she is hoping I will say? Immediate answers, born of a desire to be helpful, may be counter productive, obscuring the questions and anxieties beneath the question, and the dynamics within the system, including between therapist and family. Unpacking these may prove more helpful in the change process and actively involves everyone. Family members will have their own ideas and feelings about any question asked. Where possible, therapist responses should aim to elicit these and the underlying dynamics or processes.

Conclusion

In this chapter we have focused on the process of a session. Clearly, the focus is on 'what for' rather than 'why', on process as much as content, on relationships between people, in order to understand what is happening. Once change has begun, the 'problem' for the system becomes how to maintain it: a future orientation in which hypotheses about forces making for or impeding change and difference are crucial.

Circular questions will again be helpful in enabling people to co-construct an enabling difference, having identified the myths, anxieties or scripts which prevented it (Penn, 1985). Thus, 'Rachel, when you leave home, what do you think Freda will do?' Or, 'If Rachel does not leave home, will Freda be more or less able to go out?' Such questions point to possible sources of stuckness and yet open up the possibility of difference.

Steptoe Family Roles

Ron has always worked and, in the climate of unemployment, is very proud of this. He does not feel that the family appreciate this achievement, nor his constant anxiety of losing his job. He has been married once before, briefly. He believes that people should be able to sit in a clean house and bring friends home. He feels ashamed of the condition of the house and stigmatised in the neighbourhood and at work because of the reputation of his house. He blames his wife for this, feeling that she is lazy. When pressed he will admit to having hit her at times, kept her short of money in the hope that she will clean the house, and been angry with her because she is not interested in sex with him. He says that he loves his wife but he has had affairs which Freda knows about but prefers to keep 'secret' from the children. He believes that he could not live on his own. Ron says that this is because he would be short of money but he feels that he could not survive emotionally. In the past he has refused to attend meetings with therapists because he feels that Freda will not change. Ron believes that Rachel might benefit from a period in care because that might teach her and Freda a lesson and ensure Rachel's future school attendance. Ron is unable to help Rachel get to school because he leaves for work too early. In the evenings he spends most of his time at the local working men's club. He has no extended family. His own childhood was unhappy but has never been the subject of conversation before.

Freda feels that she has been left to raise four children as a single parent. She is angry with Ron for his behaviour and lack of understanding but she is frightened of his violence. She is in considerable debt, continually 'robbing Peter to pay Paul.' She is afraid of what will happen to Rachel, partly because she feels that Rachel is sensitive and would be harmed by being in care, and partly because Freda uses her as a go-between with Ron when she is not speaking to him. Freda would like a tidy home but feels that Ron would make fresh demands on her then. She feels depressed but gains some self-esteem by helping out at the community centre. She has tried to separate from Ron but this seems too fraught if she initiates it. Freda has no extended family and she is feeling sad at the prospect of her children growing up and leaving home. Freda is sad that Albert rarely comes home and almost never stays. But then, where would he sleep?

Albert feels angry with both his parents and has little time for them. He is home on leave currently. However, he will not be present for future sessions as he will shortly be posted abroad. He does not feel that there will be any improvement and believes that he has managed to 'get where he is today' by his efforts alone. He is staying with friends because of the mess in the house. Of all the children, Albert truanted least and can remember times when the house was clean and his parents' marriage characterised by some friendship. He tries to be loyal to both parents, seeing them equally to 'blame.'

Peter is working and spending little time at home. He leaves the house early in the morning and returns late at night. His sympathy, such as it is, lies with Ron and Peter believes that his mother should do more at home. He is angry with Marion for not helping Freda more. Peter feels that Marion is lazy. He rarely pays his 'board and lodging' money on time. He intends to leave home as soon as he can.

Marion feels very close to Freda and feels angry with Ron. She feels that Rachel should go to school and has tried to get her up in the mornings since Freda goes to bed so late to avoid Ron and then oversleeps. Marion does not help to clear up the mess, although she promises to help. She sees marriage as an escape from the home and believes that she might be pregnant. Everyone in the family knows this and both parents are furious about it. Marion has been unable to hold down a job. She is unhappy and anxious to leave home.

Rachel sees herself as the go-between for her parents and hopes that they will stay together. She says that she dislikes school and, indeed, is bullied and called names by the other children because of the reputation which her family and house have. She also finds the school work difficult. This is because she has missed a lot of school, both through truancy and the hospitalisation following the car accident when she was knocked down. Rachel is also worried about her mother. This keeps her at home and distracts her when at school. So far she has not felt able to tell either of her parents this, but only because no-one has encouraged her to do so. She wants to speak about these things and she is pleased that professionals will be seeing the family again. She does not feel that her parents understand her position. Rachel is full of optimism and actively tries to mediate in the family. She feels loyal to both parents and is angry with them both. She works hard in the family to keep the peace and to try to bring people together. She takes this role also in therapy sessions. Rachel is seen by her parents as too trusting and as vulnerable. Indeed, she is exceedingly friendly with whoever will speak to her. Her parents also see her as cheeky and boundary testing, especially about coming-in times. There is, therefore, considerable distress beneath this friendly, optimistic exterior, which Rachel has yet to feel able to share. She does not want to go into care but believes that this is likely to happen.

Chapter 5
Process Interventions

Broadly, we can divide interventions (things therapists might do in order to help a family to change) into those used in the process of a session, and those introduced in a more formal way at the end of the session, usually following a withdrawal by the therapist and discussion with the team if there is one. The first we have called process interventions, and are the subject of this chapter. The second, because they provide a bridge between sessions, we have called bridging interventions and these are dealt with in Chapter 6.

Our understanding of interventions, particularly process interventions, derives from the work done by systems theorists to understand communication. The other major consideration is that all kinds of interventions must be closely tied to the hypotheses that have been, or are being, worked out. We will lay some foundations in these areas before tackling interventions in detail.

If an hypothesis stands up to test, then we can use it to judge the effects that different things we might do would have on the family. For example, if your hypothesis includes a daughter being sexually abused, you might expect a strong reaction to an observing team or video. You might, among other things, look for opportunities to demonstrate that sharing a secret is less damaging than expected, and can give relief. Alternatively, a worker might react in other ways, perhaps by a personal investment in the belief that the priority is to ensure that perpetrators are punished, or by feeling unsure of him/herself in relation to this kind of problem, and steering discussion away from anything that might be related. Such responses would not generally be regarded as being interventions, but they are certainly likely to have effects. In fact one of the most fundamental principles of this family therapy approach is that everything that one does potentially carries a message. We want to illustrate this with a short exercise.

Exercise 5.1 (10 minutes)
Sit in pairs facing each other, and spend 3 minutes keeping eye contact but trying not to communicate. Try as hard as you can not to communicate, but at the end of the 3 minutes, take 2 minutes each to tell the other what they did communicate.

What you will have discovered is that even during the times when you were communicating least, you partner still had plenty to interpret. When you think about it, it is impossible to avoid sending some kind of message – if you sit silently, even if you leave the room, your behaviour will be given a meaning. This is usually expressed as: *One cannot not communicate.*

As we accept this, it indicates that every aspect of our work that is visible to a family may, probably does, convey a message. We could regard this as a source of anxiety, but a more useful perception is that it reveals endless opportunities to bring about change. We can use every aspect of what we do to convey messages to our families, and it is just the fact that we are aware of them, can judge or guess the effect they will have, and are doing them deliberately, that makes us call them an intervention.

The point that one cannot not communicate was made by Watzlawick, Beavin and Jackson (1967) in the context of a lengthy and informative discussion of communication. Most of what we say in this section is derived from that work, and we would urge anyone who wants to deepen their understanding of communication and systemic family therapy in general, to read that book. While on the topic of other sources, Haley (1963) discusses issues around communication in a way that is still full of useful insights and ideas, and the strategic approach has continued to develop (Fisch, Weakland and Segal, 1982).

A further claim of Watzlawick and his colleagues is that every message must be conveyed through some medium, which will carry its own message. So when we give information, it is surrounded by tones, accents, gestures, and other qualities which may amplify, qualify, or contradict the information. So we say: *Every* communication is both a communication *and* a communication about that communication.

The surrounding information, the communication about the communication we call the *metacommunication*. It stands above, or at least beside, the mundane fact and may be very rich in meaning. Most often a communication is the content of the words, spoken, while the metacommunication is the non-verbal communication. We have at our disposal a great array of facial expressions, posture, dress, eye contact, and so on. One of the simplest metacommunications we have noticed in our families is the way people lean towards or away from each other as they approve and disapprove of what the other is saying. Sometimes the statement 'we are very close' is accompanied by such a pronounced leaning away from the other that we worry that the speaker will fall off their chair.

Because it is at a different level, it follows that the metacommunication can, in subtle ways, negate the message, and so we have the conditions which make double binds possible. Let us have an everyday example. In a supermarket, a parent was heard to say to a child, in a whining voice, "shuddup bloody moaning". The overt message was clear: stop moaning. A metacommunication (in addition to "I am fed up with you") was that if you want to change someone's behaviour, you should moan at them.

Exercise 5.2 (20 minutes)
Keeping the whole group together, imagine you are interviewing your bank manager with a view to obtaining an overdraft which you say is to repair your roof. Your communication is that you can be relied on to use the loan responsibly and pay it back within the specified time. First, suggest metacommunications that would contradict the communication. Then suggest metacommunications that would reinforce the message. Make sure that in each case you have covered a good range of transient and longer lasting messages.

The prefix 'meta-' is frequently heard among systems enthusiasts. It has the implication of stepping outside or above a system so that the whole pattern can be appreciated, something that is not possible from the inside. So we have got used to speaking of a meta-perspective to describe this position. 'Going meta' has become a useful shorthand for extricating oneself from the view obtained when you are part of the system, becoming free of its influence, and being able to see it in a wider context. So a therapist who is becoming enmeshed in a family, perhaps taking one person's side, may receive a reminder from the team, or from the part of their own awareness that has stayed clear, to go meta, and will know that they have to move to a broader perspective. One direct advantage is the possibility of recognising the different levels of a double bind, and so of avoiding being trapped by it.

With this new piece of jargon established, we can now abbreviate our last aphorism to: Every communication is accompanied by a metacommunication.

In our first session with the Calderdales, several members of the family commented on Jill's bad behaviour. Jack talked of it gleefully with a sideways glance at his father, who took it up with some anger, and in a context of Jill needing correction and punishment; mother talked about Jill but gestured towards the whole family, and related it to things getting too much for her; Angela appeared frightened by what Jill was doing, and Jill herself minimised the behaviour and tried to turn attention away by a resentful reaction. All of the family were talking about the same thing, in much the same terms, but the metacommunications produced a very varied set of meanings.

Exercise 5.3 (30 minutes)
Work in pairs for this one, sharing with someone that you work with if possible. Think of your last face-to-face contact with an individual, couple or family. List five of the most important things they said; then describe the metacommunications that accompanied the message. Discuss with your partner what difference the metacommunication makes to possible interpretations of the message, and the effects it had.

Now think of the last time you were at work. List some of the metacommunications you offered your clients and your colleagues. Remember that metacommunications are not necessarily negative. They can be positive, can sweeten an otherwise unpalatable message, and are an essential component of human communication. Swap the lists. Each of you should then take 5 minutes to comment on the list you have been given. Two rules here: only comment on the metacommunications listed, not on any others that you may know are habitual; and positively connote all of them.

To sum up: everything we do during therapy is a communication and therefore at least potentially an intervention. The distinction might best be made in terms of an idea like 'leverage'. What we are looking for in therapy is something in the family that allows a relatively small input by us to bring about a significant change in the family, hence the idea of a lever. We need to establish a perception in the family which enables our communications to have an effect. If the family has decided that the therapy team is a bunch of idiots who are only interested in showing off to each other, then all leverage is lost, and however hard we work, and however insightful our interventions, everything we do will be disregarded. One of the characteristics of systemic family therapy is that the forms that interventions take are designed both to increase leverage, and to have specific effects.

Process Interventions

Interventions start at the first contact. The family will start with a set of expectations about you. Except that it is probably unstated, this set of expectations can usefully be regarded as an hypothesis. Into that hypothesis they will then fit their experience. Whoever makes the first contact will also try to get you to conform to their view of reality. 'I won't be able to get John to come' may incorporate metacommunications about the speaker deciding who comes; the problem only concerning certain members of the family; the team having to accept prior conditions etc. So the suggestions about handling first contact (Chapter 3) can now be seen to be suggested interventions. Mostly they come down to maintaining leverage by avoiding accepting preconditions, and not reinforcing an existing linear account of the problem.

As the first session starts some fundamental decisions have to be made. How will the family interpret a preliminary period of gathering baseline information about the constitution of the family? Alternatively, what metacommunication will be perceived if we launch straight into an account of 'the problem'? Already it is clear that the preliminary hypotheses are crucial and also that the way matters are handled will allow the family to develop ideas about what our hypotheses are. They will be very alert to any indication of blaming, and also to evidence that we think one member of the family is crazy. Whether they see such attitudes as a threat, or as confirmation of a cherished belief does not really matter – the point is that these are linear punctuations and our job is not to reinforce them but to offer more useful alternatives.

So let us examine some aspects of detailed operation during the session. In each case we are expecting to use the technique both to generate and test hypotheses, and to achieve our general therapeutic objectives.

Circular Questioning

The role of circular questioning in generating hypotheses has already been discussed. Let us here consider the kinds of effects it may have. When one person is asked about the perceptions of another or the relationship between two other people, this potentially opens up a number of ways of thinking. As discussed in Chapter 2, each family member will have a perception of the rest of the family, but they may not often, or ever, state their assumptions. So circular questioning puts the speaker into the position of expressing their perceptions in a very concrete way, and also conveys the message that their perception is important because the therapist thinks it is worth knowing. Then there is the response of the people described. They may be surprised by what they hear, and must be given an opportunity to say so, while the speaker may discover that certain assumptions are not after all shared by others in the family. So whenever X has been asked about Y or the relationship between Y and Z, it is essential to turn to Y and Z and check with them. This is not done in terms of 'Is X right?' because we are trying to get away from that whole idea. Rather: 'How would you describe it?'; 'Would you want to add anything to that?'; 'Is there any difference between how you and X would describe it?' and so on. Such questions are not only necessary in order to uncover differences in perception within the family. They also ensure that everyone is included, and that no-one will end up feeling disregarded, with their opinions connoted as unimportant.

Family therapy practitioners have come to realise that the techniques they have developed for conducting interviews can in themselves be very powerful. It has even been suggested that circular questioning alone may be sufficient to free a family to operate differently, and that bridging interventions will then be unnecessary. We will come back to this suggestion, but first, let us get a feel for how other techniques might be experienced.

Positive Connotation and Reframing

We have talked about positive connotation mainly in relation to hypotheses. But some version of positive connotation needs to be used throughout all contacts with the family. If the first discussion is a telephone call, it is necessary to gently deflect disparaging comments that the caller may make about their family members, and to indicate your determination to keep an open mind. One of our most powerful tools is consistently to shade what the family says into more positive terms. This will be done most productively on the basis of a clear hypothesis that fulfils all of the requirements listed in Chapter 4, but at the most detailed level, positive connoting can be a strategy throughout.

The simplest form is *reframing*. Families often habitually use quite damaging and hurtful terms to describe each others' and their own behaviour. People will talk of insult, fights, cruelty and so on. Nearly always the behaviour to which these terms refer can be described in less harmful ways. To start with a term may have to be introduced in an account of some kind to make it acceptable, e.g. "What you talk about as 'this disgusting mess' could I suppose be thought of as a kind of collection – that a person cannot bear to give up something they have acquired and so they accumulate it all – a kind of collected past that they keep always with them." Then you could go on to be interested in 'this collected past' to find out what it does to relationships in the family. In time, the family will accept this description, which then allows them to think of the rubbish not as something blameworthy that they are helpless to confront, but as something with meaning and possibility.

Exercise 5.4 (10 minutes)
Sit in pairs and take it in turns for X to describe something rotten that they know has happened (not necessarily to them), then Y must produce the best reframing they can manage. Then it is Y's turn to offer something rotten.

Now we want to introduce a few more of the important aspects of conducting a session in such a way that may give the family freedom to behave differently.

Neutrality
We have already mentioned this essential component of the Milan approach. Neutrality is about not taking sides within the family. Most obviously any overt joining of one family member can lose one the chance to influence the others who will feel rejected and blamed. The importance of neutrality was probably first recognised when early attempts were made to redress the balance in families to take pressure off the identified patient. Strenuous attempts were made to counteract the negative perceptions of the rest of the family, and in particular a lot of attention would be paid to an ignored or rejected member. The result was found to be that the isolation of the identified patient would increase. The rest of the family would resent the attention they were getting, and because the therapists were seen as being on their side

against the rest, it was easy to dismiss their perceptions. 'It's alright for you, you don't have to live with him.'

As with other aspects of this method, we have found that neutrality is not something that can be turned on and off. It has to become built into the way we interpret and discuss what we see, and a fundamental feature of our hypotheses. But isn't this unrealistic? Don't people sometimes do awful things that we simply should not be neutral about, even if we could? The issue here is not simple, and it crops up for further detailed discussion in Chapter 11 on child abuse. For the present, we would accept that it is necessary to have our own opinions and values by which we judge behaviour, but this can operate alongside the ways we think about people within families that we are working with.

It is not necessary, and certainly is not useful, to join in an exercise of symmetrical blaming, or even a complementary process in which blaming is responded to by escalating confessions of guilt.

Neutrality will be maintained by using both the general and the specific aspects of systemic working that we have already discussed. 'She is awful' should not be met by agreement, contradiction, or acceptance implied by questions like 'In what ways?'. First, our objective is to cultivate some distance that allows us to be curious. Then, we must shift the focus towards behaviour rather than moral worth, and towards the effects of the behaviour rather than an evaluation of it. So responses could be in the form:

When did you first start thinking that Y is awful?
Does Y think she is awful?
What does she do that makes you feel that she is awful?
When did she last do something like that? Can you describe what actually happened?
What happened before she did that?
Who was most upset afterwards?
What did each person do?
How does X feel when you say Y is awful? Then to X 'is that how you most often feel?'
What effect does it have on Y when you say she is awful?
What would Y have to do differently to have you no longer feel she is awful?
Would you settle for anything less than that? What is the minimum change in what Y does that would allow you to stop feeling she is awful?
Can you think of any ways we might help Y to do these things?

In such questions, the focus on people's behaviour, perceptions and feelings, together with some implicit assumptions such as the phrase 'allow you to stop' which assumes the person would stop if they could, can be very powerful. They shift the discussion away from the blaming in a way that does not join it (which would side against Y) but does not arouse resistance by contradicting it (which would side against the speaker). Instead, it is treated as an important phenomenon which needs to be explored.

Note that responding in the way suggested does not require that you have any particular opinion about the judgement. You could agree, disagree, or not bother to decide, because what you are interested in is not the awfulness of Y, but the fact that the speaker has this belief, and you want to know what consequences that belief has in the family. Neutrality, then, derives naturally from other aspects of the Milan approach. Its most general advantage is to maintain therapist manoeuvrability and leverage, but it also helps in keeping the therapist focused on systemic objectives.

Naming the Game

These interventions, which are among the simplest, work by making the family aware of the hidden or denied meaning of a behaviour. This aspect of systemic work has already been introduced in Chapter 2 in terms of offering a description of repetitive patterns within the family. Words can be very powerful in making an habitual pattern visible. Once a pattern has been pointed out, for example that whenever we start to discuss the parents' relationship someone starts paying attention to one of the children misbehaving, it is very difficult for the family to maintain the pattern into the future, without being aware of what they are doing. Describing the family's techniques for detouring problems can emerge naturally in the session if the sequence occurs during the discussion. Otherwise clues to the pattern may arise from their descriptions of events at home, which is one of the reasons why we stress the need to obtain detailed accounts of what actually happens before, during and after displays of the symptom. In this case naming the game may be best kept for the final intervention.

In either case the pattern should be described in a way that elicits curiosity rather than being accusatory. Not 'you are getting one of the children into trouble in order to avoid talking about your relationship'. Instead the family should be invited to join you in wondering about the game. 'We have noticed that there seems to be a pattern in the times that you choose for improving the behaviour of the children. So far as we can see it is much more likely to happen when . . . is going on. If we are right this could be important because the children will catch on to that kind of thing and it could affect their response to advice. Could you try not to do things differently, but whenever you find yourselves correcting the children, make a note of what was going on immediately beforehand.' More long-winded of course, but vastly more effective in removing one of the props that has enabled the system to avoid change up to now.

A further importance of naming the game arises because secrets, or an unspoken agreement never to discuss a topic, are such important components of stuck systems. Simply refusing to join in this aspect of the system can be very powerful. It is not always easy, because there can be strong pressure not to mention certain topics within a family. However we have found that whenever we have taken a deep breath and brought a topic out into the open, we have survived the experience.

And very often there has been considerable freeing up of the family immediately afterwards. Some examples are:

1) I am confused now, where in fact does your daughter sleep?
2) Does anyone in the family believe the do-it-yourself will ever be finished?
3) So what happens about sex?
4) Although you love him I wonder if there are times when you wish Daddy would go away?
5) Is that a bite mark on Jane's arm?

The reason that naming the game is so effective is that secrets have often acquired a circular life of their own. It is almost as if the only reason for not mentioning something is that it is a secret, and we know it is a secret because nobody ever talks about it. All that is required is to talk about the topic in a safe, matter-of-fact way and avoid being struck down by a thunderbolt. Then the circular process that sustained the secret is punctured and the family discover that it can be dealt with after all.

Focus on behaviour/the problem

These aspects of working with families have already been fully discussed in Chapter 4. Here we just want to remind you of how powerful such insistence can be. 'What was the latest thing he did that made you think "he is uncontrollable"?' can have powerful consequences. Quite often, after a variety of non-specific answers ('almost everything' etc.) have been met with a repeat of the question, we are told 'Well, he has been a lot better recently'. Sometimes a behaviour is described and on exploration the last occasion was months or even years ago. In one of our families 'the fits' which were believed to be the cause of many problems turned out to be two fits, the latest of which had occurred eight years ago.

An insistence on a precise statement of what kind of a problem it is for each member of the family, often uncovers substantial discrepancies. Most commonly, each will deny it is a problem for them, but that it has to be stopped because it is upsetting someone else. Even if there are not outright contradictions, defining the problem tends to make it much more manageable and allows the family to realistically judge how much change is needed.

Splitting the team

A final specific technique, if there are at least two of you, is to model the possibility of alternative stories. We quite often use messages in the form 'some of the team were suggesting that Jill goes off at night so that Mum and Dad will have to get together to go out looking for her. I am not sure about that because I had been thinking that she goes off because there is something happening at home that she can't bear, and she doesn't want to get into a fight over it. Can we talk about the two ideas and see whether either of them is helpful – or maybe both of them have some truth in them.'

From messages like this the family can learn that there may be alternative stories, all of which may be useful, and that even 'experts' can have different perceptions, but that they don't have to compete about them.

Further process interventions are described in Chapter 7, but the set described here will take you a long way, so let us take stock.

The Objectives of Family Therapy

We can now begin to make sense of thinking of therapy activity as an intervention in terms of the objectives of the consultation. As a core summary, we have families coming with a problem that they have a strong tendency to think about in certain ways. Our view is that it is these very tendencies that prevent them from finding a way of living that they would all prefer. Typically they see the problem as resulting from the characteristics of one person; they feel that if only that person would change everything would be alright, but they have tried to change the person and have discovered that they cannot so they are feeling helpless. Our assumption is that the symptom is at least as much an adaptation to other problems in the family as it is the cause of them. If we can get the family to accept this aspect then there is suddenly much more scope for things to change. We could put a list of typical family perceptions into a Table along with the alternative perceptions that we want to develop:

Table 5.1 Therapeutic objectives as a shift in clients' perceptions

INITIAL PERCEPTIONS OF PROBLEM	OBJECTIVE
located in individual	arising from the system
uncontrollable/unchangeable	temporary
intrinsic	accidental
blameworthy	redundant
sinister	well-meaning but mistaken
linear	circular
partisan	neutral

With this kind of perspective in mind, we are in a position to notice every communication or metacommunication that preserves the initial perceptions, and to use our methods to move it towards our objectives.

Exercise 5.5 (15 minutes)
In a group, take it in turns to make one statement about the Calderdale family which fits the left hand column of Table 5.1. Then discuss how a therapist could have responded to rephrase the statement in terms of the right hand column, without directly confronting or contradicting the perception.

Exercise 5.6 (45 minutes)
This exercise works best in groups of about nine. We want to set up a role-play of the Steptoes, so five (or six if the group is more than nine) people to play the family should stop reading at this point, go and read up the family roles (at the end of Chapter 4), and get into role by discussing the problem of the mess in the house.

The remainder of the group should now work on formulating circular questions. The first step is to agree one or more hypotheses, then to identify essential information that would enable the hypothesis to be tested or elaborated. Then the form of circular questioning must be decided. Issues to be covered might include: who gets their way most; who gets on best – in pairs/with Rachel/with the absent brother; how does Ron and Freda's relationship change when others are present; how is education viewed in the family.

The difference between this exercise and the role-play in Chapter 4 is that here we want you to bring in as many as possible of the ideas we have introduced as process interventions. This will be difficult the first time, and so the therapists will need active help.

Now choose two therapists to ask the questions, with the rest as 'shadows' sitting behind them to suggest more circular ways of obtaining information, remind the therapists of the hypothesis and generally be helpful. It is important for the shadows to feel free to interrupt, especially just after a question has been asked. Once it has been stated, one of you may see a way in which it could be rephrased so that it is more neutral, positive, or circular. Or you may be able to use it to practise naming the game, reframing, or splitting the team. Do not worry if the process feels rather artificial, the important thing is to explore just how far you can convert your questioning so that it becomes an intervention. Do this for half an hour.

While in role, the family should be questioned (circularly preferably), about how they experienced the session. What we are particularly interested in is whether the constant use of process interventions made it more difficult for them to maintain their patterns of blaming and hopelessness. Table 5.1 can be used as a checklist for the kind of shift in perceptions that we would hope for.

Now de-role, therapists as well as family.

You may wish, perhaps in a later session, to reverse roles so that the 'family' have a chance to practise process interventions. In that case, use the Calderdales as a family to role-play, and repeat this exercise.

Conclusion

We have been discussing ways of using the way the session is conducted as a deliberate intervention. Now that the power of these aspects of systemic working can be appreciated, a more fundamental aspect can be recognised. If we conducted a session in a non-systemic way we might be successful in generating the information we need for our hypotheses and to formulate a bridging intervention. But the questioning will have substantial effects on the family, whichever style is adopted. If the approach is purely non-directive, or uncondítonally supportive of whoever speaks, or inquisitorial or aggressive, the family will reach the end of the session with well established perceptions of the therapy and expectations through which they will interpret the final intervention. Only if the whole conduct of the session has been consistently systemic, can a systemic bridging intervention have its maximum effect.

Chapter 6
Bridging Interventions

As described in Chapter 5, the earlier idea of Milan family therapy was that it relied almost entirely for its effect on an intervention at the end of the session. The session itself was taken up with developing a reliable hypothesis, which was then used in the team discussion as a basis for constructing an intervention which is then delivered to the family just before they leave. Often the intervention consisted of a story, in which the meaning of the symptom was recast, and then an instruction to the family to engage in a prescribed activity – usually a ritual in which all of the family would have a role. The report of the family at the next session about what had happened then provides information for generating new hypotheses. The book which inspired much of the growth of Milan systemic family therapy, particularly in Britain during the 1980s (Selvini Palazzoli, Boscolo, Cecchin and Prata, 1978) was based very largely on bridging interventions. When the original team split up, Palazzoli's group researched the idea of standard interventions, and this idea was developed by de Shazar (1986). His idea is that a symptom is like a locked door, and while it may be interesting to know about the construction of the door, why it is locked, and so on, if you want to open it all you need is a skeleton key. If we could find skeleton keys for family problems that would unlock any symptom, then therapy could be quicker and easier. Our experience suggests that this idea has to be classified under 'it would be nice if things worked like that, but they don't'. Many of de Shazar's ideas are interesting and the two 'keys' he suggests are sometimes useful, but the book is mainly interesting as an example of reliance on bridging interventions.

This model is still used, but we no longer place such weight on the final intervention. The recognition that what we have called process interventions can have a powerful effect on the family removes the feeling that everything hangs on the effectiveness of the prescription at the end of the session. However these prescriptions are often extremely useful, so this chapter is devoted to techniques of formulating and delivering them.

When we first saw the clinical work of the Milan team there was something magical about their interventions. Even films which seemed to show the whole process including the team discussion gave no indication of how the formulation was discovered. With time and experience the process has become much clearer, and in our thinking the answer has turned out to be almost absurdly simple. When we sat down to discuss the characteristics that an intervention must have, we produced the following list:

Table 6.1 Requirements of a good intervention

	A good intervention:
1	Is circular
2	Is about relationships
3	Is expressed in terms of what people do and believe, rather that what they are
4	Preserves therapist neutrality
5	Includes all members of the family system
6	Positively connotes everyone
7	Is meta to the family's hypothesis
8	Contains an assumption, but not a demand, for change

This table should look familiar because it is until the last item the same as the list in Chapter 4 of the requirements for a systemic hypothesis. So the fundamental answer is that interventions come from hypotheses.

What is an intervention required to do? Here again we can refer back to a previous Table (5.1) of therapeutic objectives. The effect of the intervention should be to help shift the perceptions of family members towards the right hand column. Bridging interventions, though, can be rather more ambitious, and here we would refer back to Chapter 2 and the spiral Figure (2.2). The systemic view is that processes such as symmetrical and complementary responses have resulted in an extreme state as the attempted solution is escalated to its limits. In that example, the limits were reached when mother felt she could not increase her pressure, and the son had withdrawn as far as he could, without incurring other costs for example, physical illness.

Once a system has reached a stable state, at the limit of what is tolerable, the people within it start to feel vulnerable. There is a sense of precariousness because any reduction in the 'solution' will allow the problem to surface, and any increase will be intolerable. In these circumstances the people not only feel trapped, they will vigorously resist any direct attempt to bring about change. They will say they want things to be different, but they will feel unable to do anything differently. The task of an intervention is to unhook the family from its rather precarious stability. But even in our simple example we can expect this to be resisted.

Asking mother to stop pressuring her son and leave him to find his own level of activity will be a waste of time. For one thing, plenty of people including the son and probably the mother herself have given her this advice in the past. And how could a conscientious and worried mother abandon her son in this way? Similarly, inviting the son totally to change his lifestyle on the promise that this will result in his mother totally changing her behaviour will look like an impossible task and a great risk. Another feature of these direct attempts to produce change is that they carry a number of messages. They are saying 'try our version of reality and you will find it works better'. To accept this, the couple would have to accept our version on trust; that their version had been wrong; that their suffering had been unnecessary; and their behaviour unreasonable. We find that people tend to find such a package unattractive.

Exercise 6.1 (10 minutes)
Think of the last attempt that you made to bring about change in a system, which was ineffectual – either with clients or colleagues. Try to see, from the perspective of the other people, what extra implications they would have had to accept. Exaggerate freely, just to get an idea of why some of these metacommunications might have appeared unacceptable to them.

You should do it differently = you have been doing it wrong
It will be easy = how pathetic that you didn't do it already
My way is better = your way is worse
You will be good if you do it this way = you have been bad to do it that way.
I have a good idea = I am cleverer than you

So a systemic intervention needs to enable people to give up their solution without having to accept a lot of negative implications. Fortunately the systemic view provides a direct way of doing this. Since we see the symptom/problem as having grown out of a well-intentioned attempt to solve a problem within the family (a redundant adaptation, in other words) it should be possible for us to understand and describe the current situation in terms that do not demand an acceptance of guilt and inadequacy from the family.

Providing an acceptable systemic account of the problem, that is an hypothesis, is something that is done for the use of the therapist – it is not necessarily going to free up the system on its own. So telling the family our hypothesis may form part of an intervention but it is unlikely to be enough. The additional ingredient is to make it difficult for the existing pattern to continue. In systems terms this means making the solution ineffective, either by changing the perceived meaning of some behaviour, or by making it necessary for behaviour to be escalated beyond tolerable limits.

We will now consider various forms that bridging interventions may take.

Naming the Game

This kind of intervention has already been extensively discussed, but a bridging intervention gives scope for a more detailed form.

A recent example of part of one of our interventions (not verbatim) indicates the style: "The family has some standard ways of behaving which have become very familiar, and although everyone complains about them, they seem to be something you all fall back on from time to time. One of them is that everyone in the family knows how to provoke Paul (aged 3 years). We have noticed that when something uncomfortable is being discussed, someone will set Paul off and he will then do one of his naughty tricks. Then everyone gets cross with him, and forgets to carry on with the uncomfortable discussion. We have seen several families that have managed to keep the peace under severe difficulties in this kind of way, so it would not be surprising if something of the kind was happening here.

However, it is always worth knowing if that is what is going on because we can then find ways of making it easier for the children. So we have been wondering if this is one of the ways you avoid serious disagreements at home. What we would like you to do is all to watch out over the next month to see whether this kind of thing happens. But, because we think this familiar pattern is very important in preventing serious conflict, we do not want you to do anything to change it. Just watch out for when it happens, and come back and let us know."

Our expectation is that by making the family aware of the sequence, it will be impossible for it to continue in its previous concealed and powerful form. Provoking Paul will lead at least some of the family to suspect that some issue is being avoided.

Take Away the Constraints

We have pointed out that a system may achieve stability when all of the tendencies run up against some external limit. In the simple mother-son example, as discussed above, there may have been simple physical limits on any further escalation. But what would happen if we managed to override one of those limits? Suppose the family could accept a story that accepted their judgement that the symptom is an unavoidable and essential aspect of their lives, and therefore that they should spend all their time and energy on it? Once the external limits have been removed, they may discover that they do not wish to continue the behaviour. Alternatively, they will each have to accept that they are choosing how much to do.

Take Away the Mutual Support

Within a system, any piece of behaviour or belief can only be sustained because it is supported by other parts of the system. Some of the most important methods are described in Chapter 2. In our example, mother's 'nagging' is kept up by son's 'laziness' which is made necessary by mother's nagging. It follows that if the reciprocal behaviour is removed, the first behaviour cannot be kept going.

The idea here is very much like that at the basis of Judo: if someone is pushing hard against you, they come to rely on you for their balance. If you remove your resistance, they will be obliged to find their own balance to avoid falling forwards. But in Judo you do not *just* stop pushing back otherwise you will be pushed over. You also have to side-step so that the force of your opponent's push moves them and not you. Then *they* have to find a way of pulling back on their own. Here the comparison ends because in Judo you would help them on their way whereas in family therapy we are happy that they should regain their balance. So an intervention has to remove support from the symptom by enabling others to side-step its effects. The commonest way of doing this is to offer an alternative perception in which the symptom changes from being an outcome that the family is powerless to prevent, to being a cause that has up to now been needed for the effects it has. For example, staying in bed enables mother to show her concern, which she thinks he has needed up to now. Constant pressure gives him an opportunity to respond by staying in bed, so that he does not go off from home, which he thinks will be too threatening for mother.

Presenting the Hypothesis

A good systemic hypothesis can be a powerful tool for change in its own right. Often it will need relatively little change to be presented to the family. From the list of Table 6.1, the ingredient to add is an orientation to the future. This is important because otherwise an hypothesis may reinforce the tendency of a stuck family to relive the past or be totally focused on the present. The hypothesis should lead naturally to an indication of how things might be different, since it is explicit about how they are at present being kept the same. Reference to the future often has an element of naming the game, since it may be fear of the future that is keeping the system fixed. Casual reference to 'some time in the future when all the children have left home' or 'when Craig no longer feels he has to have tantrums' mentions the unmentionable and brings it within the realm of topics that must be considered. But in order to prevent this being threatening, it is essential not to impose a time scale or demand progression towards it. Keeping it in the future, at a time that the family will decide is appropriate, gives hope without arousing the threat that giving up the problem poses.

Although presenting the hypothesis more or less straight can be effective it is not always the best use of the material. So when you have come up with a really good hypothesis, do not rush in to give it to the family. First look to see what else you might do with it. It should offer various ideas for intervening and these may offer more leverage while generating more information than the polite way in which the telling of the hypothesis is received.

Rituals

Prescribing a ritual is a powerful tool for change in a family. A ritual is a task which is carried out by designated members of the family in a carefully prescribed way and a specified time and place. The purpose as with all interventions is to make it difficult for the family to continue with their current solution, but this is usually achieved in rituals by challenging some family belief or myth. If a family belief is that the children will go out of control if the parents go out and leave them, then the parents may be sent to the cinema. If the myth is that children must be protected from failure at all costs (and so they are never offered any challenges) the children can be asked to suggest something that they could be sure to fail at, and then do it trying as hard as they can, but knowing that they are expected to fail. If the sky will fall in if Jane says what she thinks about grandmother, then Jane can be instructed to make up the worst things she can think of about grandmother, and everyone is to applaud the particularly wild statements.

It will have occurred to you that families might balk at doing some of these tasks, and so they might. For this reason the form and presentation must be carefully thought through. Rituals must be presented within a story that makes sense to the family. As far as possible the story is told in words and concepts that the family themselves use, and the task must make sense to them. So having the children fail might be put within a context of the splendid job that the parents had done to protect them from failure, but our concern is that the parents will not be able to protect them for ever, so they will inevitably encounter failure at some time, and will not have the experience to cope with it. So it would be much better if they were to get some experience of failure while the parents are there to make sure it is not harmful to them. If the ritual fails because it turns out that the children could manage the tasks after all, a further myth will have been demolished.

Making the Symptom Worse

In the spirit of reversing the push, it is sometimes useful to think of what could be done to make matters worse. If we suspect that the symptom – tantrums say – is being maintained by the efforts to prevent it, then the family could be asked, at prescribed times, to see whether they could provoke a tantrum. More generally they could be asked to try a variety of things and see which were effective in making the symptom worse, or just to discuss what they would do if they really wanted more of the symptom. There are two possible useful outcomes from this. First, the family may discover that there is a remarkable similarity between what they would do to make things worse and what they do to try to prevent it. Secondly, the intervention may fail because they cannot produce the symptom. It is difficult wholeheartedly to provide your symptom if everyone is looking on asking you to do it. And if your role until now has been to do the opposite of what is asked, then you may find that you are automatically refusing to comply with attempts to make you have the symptom.

Finally, two aspects of intervention that were frequently discussed in earlier books on Milan family therapy.

Prescribing the Symptom

Many interventions have an element of this idea. Asking for the symptom to be produced to order has a number of interesting features. It reverses the usual pressure for change; contradicts the idea that the symptom is some kind of disaster that must be prevented at all costs; possibly reduces excitement about the symptom and instead connotes it as something of interest about which one can afford to be curious. Prescribing the symptom is likely to be done within the context of indicating that it plays an important role in the family. Finally, there is an element of paradox, given Haley's definition of a symptom (Chapter 2). If it is something you cannot help, then producing it to order challenges that belief. But if you do not produce it, you have to abandon the idea that it cannot be prevented.

Prescribing the symptom is still an effective component of many interventions. At the least, a prescription of 'no change' figures quite often. One derivation that we have found to be effective is to ask a family to hold discussions about which aspects of their family they would not want to change. Apart from the advantage of taking them by surprise, and disrupting the set with which they have come for help, the responses can be very informative. Occasionally we have been surprised by the vehemence with which total change has been demanded but much more often the family themselves are surprised to find how much is valued by each other. The task also indicates areas of strength that can be built on in the future.

Counter-Paradox

The first major publication of the Milan group was called 'Paradox and Counter-Paradox' and had an enormous impact. The basic concept is that families get stuck because they have become trapped in a paradox, and that the solution lies in presenting a therapeutic paradox which neutralises the original. 'Paradoxical prescriptions' became almost a symbol of commitment to the Milan method, and one suspects that there was an element of machismo in the courage with which destructive behaviours were paradoxically requested. Progressively the dangers of ill-considered paradox became added to an awareness of their limitations, and they are now used much less routinely. One change may be the application of family therapy to a much wider range of situations. In the past we saw predominantly families with long-standing difficulties that had resisted attempts at resolution by various agencies. Today, a referral to family therapy, or the application of family therapy within an agency, may happen much sooner after the identification of a problem, and many of the families we now see are not trapped in an overwhelming paradox or double bind, and can be helped by much more straightforward methods.

A Sample Intervention

An intervention that might be offered to the mother and son introduced in Chapter 2 is given here.

Exercise 6.2 (20 minutes)
Read the intervention and, in groups of four, see which of the different aspects of interventions that have been discussed so far you can recognise.

"Mother needs son to show his need for her by only being active when she forces him to, and son needs mother to prove that she is still looking after him by her attempts to persuade him to get up. Only once you are both quite convinced that you can rely on the other, will you be able to move on to looking after yourself. In order to speed this process up, we want you (son) to try as hard as you can to stay in bed all the time. Just get up for basic needs and then go straight back to bed. We know this will become uncomfortable and depressing, and that you will have to give up any idea of doing new things that might interest you, but your mother really needs you to do this for a while. While he is doing this we want you (mother) to keep showing your concern by continually telling him what he should do, even though, for the time being, you know that this will have no effect because we have told him not to change. But unless he knows you are still concerned, he may not be able to keep up his side of the bargain, so however difficult and exhausting it becomes, we do want you to keep it up continuously. When you come back next month and tell us how it has gone, we will then see if you can judge how much longer you will have to keep it up before you are sure enough of each other to stop."

Aspects of the intervention that you might have noticed are as follows. The nagging and withdrawing are reframed in various ways. More basically the whole direction of cause and effect is reversed: no longer that the individual's behaviour is caused by the other, but the behaviour is what makes the other feel they have to behave in that way. The familiar and expected demands to stop the behaviour do not occur, instead they are asked to carry on. They are not blamed for what they have been doing, but are told it was being done for the sake of the other. The cost to each of them is indicated, but as a sacrifice on behalf of the other, not as a self-inflicted wound. The contribution of both is described as being in the service of a valued objective, and an indication is given that this objective can be obtained in less costly ways. By asking them to do more, the behaviour is assumed to be under their control, but this assumption is embedded in a complete account and so is not likely to provoke rejection. Change is not requested, rather they are asked to carry on as before only more so. Relinquishing the behaviour in the future is assumed, and it is indicated that the couple will be able to judge when it will be possible. But no time scale is imposed.

Taken together our hope is that these characteristics will enable each of them to accept an alternative perception of their own and the other's behaviour and intentions. In fact we are not demanding that they relinquish their previous understanding, merely that they add ours as an alternative perspective with some validity – in current terminology, laying a new story alongside the original. If they can enrich their perceptions in this way, then they will be freed from the aspects (listed in the first column of Table 5.1) which make them controlled by their relationship rather than in control of it.

Exercise 6.3 (45 minutes)
The time has come to practise formulating interventions of your own. For the exercises we will use the Calderdale and Steptoe families. As we have stressed, an intervention must follow directly from an hypothesis so let us start from the hypothesis provided at *Figure 1* of Chapter 4 for the Steptoes.

In groups of four, work through the types and aspects of bridging interventions and for each, decide how you would interpret it in relation to the hypothesis, then write down the component of an intervention that this would provide. Allow 20 minutes for this.

Next, see how you could coordinate as many of the components as possible into a coherent written intervention. Construct this intervention as if you were sending it to the family as a letter to be read out at a fixed time. Allow 15 minutes for this.

Now check that the intervention fits all of the requirements in Table 6.1. If not that is very useful because it facilitates an important piece of learning. Look at the aspects and see if there was a systemic inadequacy in your perception that was the reason. For example, if one member of the family was left out, then your hypothesis must have been incomplete because no member of a family has zero effect on any aspect of its functioning.

If your intervention was perfect do not worry. You will have plenty of opportunity for practice with later attempts.

Delivering the Intervention
When a bridging intervention is offered at the end of a family therapy session, we have learned that it is most effective if we treat it respectfully and present it in certain ways.

We write the intervention down. There are several advantages to this procedure. It adds weight to the intervention, which can be seen to be a product of the team, and not just the invention of the therapist. It indicates that it has been carefully considered, and is thought by us to be worth the effort of getting it right. It also does help to ensure that we do get it right. Complex interventions often involve saying something that is easily muddled, or that is rather confrontational. aving a written version reduces the risk that the message will be diluted. Finally it guarantees that we have a written record to refer to for the next session.

The intervention should be delivered in a slow, steady, and clear voice. If it is interrupted (say by a child demanding attention) then it should be repeated.

Elaboration should be avoided. Requests for elaboration should be met with a reasonable but firm statement on the lines that the message was carefully constructed by the team because they thought that the most useful thing until the next session would be for the family to struggle with/try out/discuss/or whatever, the precise ideas we have written down. If the family really has difficulty in taking in the message (and this can easily happen with complex stories) we prefer to offer to post a typed version than to become involved in a dialogue over it.

The intervention should be the last thing the family hear so that the impact is not diluted in any way. Our practice is to make the next appointment before the intervention. As soon as they have finished reading it the therapist stands up, says goodbye, and leaves the room. Another member of the team (the 'secretary') then comes in to show the family out.

Exercise 6.4 (20 minutes)
Take the written intervention which was planned as a letter, and use it to practise the delivery of an intervention. For this you will need to have a group to role-play the family, with one therapist delivering the intervention. Then the therapist can swop with a family member who can deliver the intervention again. By the time everyone has delivered it you will all have a detailed feeling for what is involved.

Finally, a bridging intervention must always be picked up at the start of the next session. The intervention is likely to have had an effect even if the family failed to carry out the instructions. To this extent, it is a new system that comes for the next session, so the task of constructing a new hypothesis to comprehend them must start over again. The team should have set up at least one hypothesis about how the system would be changed by the intervention in advance – ideally just after the family left from the previous session, while the events are still fresh in memory. When the next session starts, the use the family have made of the intervention is an obvious starting point for testing that hypothesis and allowing the family to surprise you by having changed in some totally unpredictable way. Use circular questions to explore exactly what people did. Who suggested the time to get together to do it; who was most/next most enthusiastic/worried about doing it. If they had done it, what would grandfather be likely to predict would have happened.

Conclusion

We have now covered the basic material needed to use this model of family therapy. We have in fact also covered many of the more advanced and recent ideas, but in the techniques we have kept to those that are essential for getting started. Also, as we have throughout the book, we have kept to practices which are tried and tested. You should now be in a position to start applying systemic family therapy ideas in your work. You may wish to set up further role-plays using your own material, or find other ways of simulating the approach, for example by working through a current case and considering how you would have handled it differently if you had been working systemically.

We will now move on to expanding your repertoire of concepts and methods in a chapter on therapist's tools.

Chapter 7
Therapist's Tools

We have now covered most of the fundamental procedures of this approach to family therapy. In this chapter we will introduce a variety of techniques and ideas which we know are useful in practice. One of the features of this approach is that it encourages inventiveness among practitioners including finding out what their colleagues are up to. It includes incorporating new ideas that look interesting from other teams into existing practice.

As a result there is available a considerable store of methods or tools which have been introduced over time, worked through with different families and different problems, and survived the test of being used in different settings.

The therapist's tools that we intend to describe here fall under three headings. The first heading relates to *tools for understanding*. As the major task of family therapy is to generate hypotheses, it is natural that the first set of tools we introduce here were developed as a way of getting better, novel, or just different insights into how families work.

The next stage in the process is to conduct the session in such a way as to test, expand, or replace the original hypotheses, to open up possibilities for change in the family, and perhaps to create a bridging intervention, so our next heading is *tools for action*. We recognise that systemic thinking can be difficult, and various ways have been proposed to help improve the work of systemic therapists at all stages; so our final section in this chapter is *tools for us*.

Tools for Understanding

It will by now be clear that an understanding of how a family functions as a system can only be obtained through a knowledge of the understandings of each person in the family. In various ways, all of the topics we cover in this section have been developed to help us understand how people, events, and relationships are perceived within the family. Myths and related concepts help us to recognise essential aspects of the family belief system; Triangles describe a tool for use in our own thinking and to help structure our understanding of relationships within the family; Mirroring uses team processes as a source of information about the family; and Geneograms are a direct route to obtaining information that may appear simple and factual but which is surprisingly rich and can often be extended into visualising a dynamic system.

Myths, Scripts and Premises

The tendency of families to develop idiosyncratic belief systems was introduced in Chapter 2, and now we want to extend this discussion. Family mythology can include stories about previous generations or absent members which provide a colourful backdrop to the family drama and which help to shape the family's identity. The disreputable uncle George who is never mentioned but somehow figures as an awful warning of the dangers, and sophisticated excitements, that threaten in the outside world. The riches, reputation, or poverty of previous generations that enrich the present ordinariness of the family. The brother who emigrated and is no doubt very successful, and the reason he has not made contact since he left, is that he feels guilty about what he said to Mabel before he left. Sometimes events within the life span of the family achieve a mythical significance. When family members have been involved in a war or similar historic event, the vividness and significance may increase over the years and become an important part of the identity of the family. All of these kinds of beliefs provide the basis of expectations that family members have about each other, and their predictions of what will happen when the family interacts with the outside world.

Myths may be in the form of beliefs about certain kinds of people, for example based on gender. One family had a traditional myth about gender roles which seemed relatively ordinary. Men go out into the world and the woman's place is in the home. The problem was that in order to preserve the myth in the face of contrary pressure from outside, the mother and daughter became agoraphobic and hardly left the house at all. Yet again, in this highly summarised example, we see a reversal of causality. The family come saying that the agoraphobia is stopping the women from going out, when the more useful story is that the agoraphobia enables them not to go out and so is needed in order to prevent a myth being challenged.

The first task of the therapist is to see past the family's story to develop an hypothesis about the underlying myth. To do this we are likely to need information from a wider perspective than the events surrounding the symptom. In the example, it was a repetitive theme in the stories the family told about family life, and the accounts of gender role across generations that provided the clues. Once the myth is identified it should not be challenged directly. It was after all a potential challenge to the myth that made it seem necessary for the women to become incapacitated. The myth can be weakened by being named and brought into the open for discussion, and alternative patterns of behaviour can be suggested that do not challenge the myth directly. A common technique is to discuss a person's loyalty to an idea, as it is more acceptable to abandon this kind of loyalty when loyalty to a person is the alternative.

Exercise 7.1 (30 minutes)
In groups of four, take 20 minutes to construct a bridging intervention to the family with the agoraphobic women which tackles the consequences of their myth without directly challenging it.

As a full group, compare your interventions. Is there a sense in which they are all the same solution? (Not necessarily a bad thing, but something to be alert for). Did each group check them against Table 5.1? If they do not check out completely, is this because you did not insist on a clearly stated hypothesis before constructing the intervention?

---

*If the way you did this exercise indicates that there is difficulty in following our approach, this might be a good time to have a discussion on what would help you to follow our guidelines more closely for a while. We make this suggestion not because we are enslaved by a myth that the approach offered in this book is the only one possible, nor that it would be impossible to improve it. But it is our experience that any technique can only be acquired effectively by practising it fairly rigorously for a time, and we would strongly urge you to stick close to the method until you are comfortable with it before becoming selective about how you use it.

Here we offer a fairly lengthy intervention which you might like to compare with the ones you have created:

"In this family we see that each of you has a clear perception of how the others want to see you. John acts in ways that prove to Mary (wife) and Jane (daughter) that he can be depended on to provide for the family and protect it from the outside world. It seems to us that whatever John might want to do, he always thinks first whether it might contradict the beliefs and wishes of Mary and Jane. The things he does make it look as if he is extremely worried about the anxiety and disappointment he would cause if he was not so strong and dependable.

In a similar way, Mary and Jane seem to have always behaved as if John needed them to play a part that balances his contribution. For him to be strong and dependable, they must not be too competent, but must rely on John for many things. Over the years, these patterns have become a bit exaggerated, with John ending up dutifully doing all of the jobs that involve the outside world, and Mary and Jane dutifully staying at home. This idea of how men should be and how women should be, has been an important factor in how well your family worked for so many years. But it does seem that it is now preventing each of you from doing what you want. And none of you can see how to give it up without causing anxiety and disappointment within the family.

At the moment, the biggest risk might be if the agoraphobia was suddenly cured. Then there would be nothing to stop Mary and Jane from going out and doing what they want: Mary might get a job, Jane would probably want to go out with friends, find a boyfriend and before long might even be thinking of leaving home. But this would leave John with a big problem because the family would not need him to make the contribution that he has until now. So before the agoraphobia can safely be given up, we think there is some work to do. The family needs to decide what John might do if Mary and Jane did not depend on him so much, and what Mary might do if John did not need her to depend on him. Then we have to think what Jane might do if her parents were giving her a different kind of example. We would want to be sure that she was given an example of being loyal to the family, even if particular ideas like how men and women ought to behave change over the years, and everyone feels more able to do their own thing.

So we see lots of complications that might possibly arise if things were to change too fast. We will need to have a number of sessions here to explore these possible complications before we would ask you to change, but until the next session, it would be useful if you could have some discussions in the following way:

Once a week, sit at your table with John and Mary on one side and Jane on the other. First, Mary should tell John her ideas about things that Jane might like to do if she felt free and did not have to worry about what her parents thought. Then John is to tell Mary his ideas on the same subject. Then all three of you should have a discussion about whether Jane would really like to do these things.

On a different day, again sit at your table with John and Mary on one side and Jane on the other. To start with, Jane should say what she thinks John, and Mary, might each like to do if they did not have to worry about the family. Then John and Mary should discuss these ideas to see whether each could imagine the other behaving in that way.

When you come back in four weeks time, we would like you to tell us what ideas came up for new things that each of you could do. But let us remind you, please, that this is just an exercise, we do not want any of you going off and doing these things until we all know that everyone would feel safe about them."

With a complicated intervention like this we would usually have it typed and sent to the family straight after the session. At the next session, each person could be asked to suggest new things they would like to do, and the other two would be asked whether this would make 'her less of a woman'/'him less of a man' in their eyes.

A final point, Byng-Hall (1988) reminds us that professional systems can also develop their own mythology. Sometimes this can become a closed belief system, just as it can in families, and so be impervious to contrary evidence. If therapists find themselves working to a formula, or becoming reluctant to question what they do, it is probably time to call in a consultant (see Chapter 10).

Scripts differ from myths in that they directly prescribe the action to be taken. Again the task of the therapist is to consider a reversal of the family's linear punctuation, and deduce the underlying script from the repeated patterns of behaviour. Boscolo, Cecchin, Campbell and Draper (1985), talk of the related concept of a 'basic premise' that the family may hold. A premise may be that everybody has to be happy, or that one must be in control and the others controlled, or that the family protects its members from a hostile external world. As Boscolo points out (p.278), if you have recognised the premise (or script) then you can change things at the lower level of everyday behaviour in a way that starts to modify the premise. If you have not recognised the premise, then your interventions will only have an effect at the lower level.

Triangles and Triangulation

The idea of recognising triangular relationships within families might be seen as a stage in a progression to true systems thinking. For most of their history, psychotherapy, medicine, and psychology have concentrated on the individual. Slowly and painfully, each discipline has come to recognise the importance of relationships, but in each case most of the effort has been expended on couples. Whether the dyad is a mother and infant, a couple in partnership, or the relationship between a doctor and a patient, consideration rarely extended to third parties. Most recently there have been some attempts to cope with threesomes, and in family therapy the idea of conceptualising relationships in terms of triangles has certainly been very helpful.

Becvar and Becvar (1988) describe a typical family triangle which can be summarised as follows: a peripheral father, an overinvolved mother and a rotten kid. The rotten kid winds mother up to the point that father becomes disturbed and enters the situation to put a stop to the child's behaviour. Mother feels he is being too strict and compensates her son by extra affection, which makes it impossible for her to control him in the future. Father retreats feeling excluded by the relationship between mother and son, and that his attempts at fathering have been undermined, mother reinforces her belief that she is ineffective, and the kid is offered no reason to behave any differently in future. This can of course go on *ad infinitum*.

Triangulation refers to the pattern in which a third person is used to resolve a problem in a dyadic relationship. In the above example, the kid is being used to maintain some interaction between the parents who otherwise could stay entirely separate. The damaging nature of such triangulation is that each person is defined in terms of their role in relation to the other two. Father is a bad father who is best staying out of things, mother is ineffectual and the kid is rotten.

In families it is usually one or more of the children who are triangulated, and we have already talked of conflict being detoured through the children (Chapter 4) which may be one of the reasons why triangulation occurs in a family. In these circumstances a child can be put into the position of being an ally of one parent and therefore against the other. In a reconstituted family, the 14 year old boy allied with his father against his step-mother. Father used this alliance to reduce the impact of the marital relationship on his lifestyle, but eventually the conflict between son and step-mother threatened the marriage. At this point the parental alliance became threatened and resulted in the son being seen as trying to wreck the family through his fights with his step-mother. The escalation of this scenario led to a referral and the family came for therapy to get help in making him more co-operative. The initial stage of therapy, which enabled the boy to feel safer and to start negotiating with his step-mother provoked a return to the triangular pattern in which the differences between the couple began to surface, and the boy was again needed to carry and represent the conflict.

As is often the case, bringing in new people (like family therapists) to relieve the stress, merely returned the problem to an earlier stage from which the process could start all over again.

Triangles have figured particularly in Minuchin's structural approach (see Chapter 1), and much of his work is expressed in terms of boundaries. Minuchin assumes that certain kinds of structure are preferable, most obviously that there should be boundaries that mark off a parental sub-system from the sub-system of children. Confusion of these boundaries, typically when a child takes on some of the parental roles, is a major source of problems, but the pattern may be fiercely defended because it is seen as protecting the family from some worse disaster. Similar concepts have been developed by Furniss (1983a) to describe the situation in families in which incest has become established. Malan (1979) has made extensive use of the image of a triangle in exploring the relationships in psychodynamic psychotherapy. All of these sources have valuable ideas that can be used to enrich a systemic understanding, but we will leave it to you to pursue triangles further if you wish.

Mirroring

The metaphor of the mirror has been used in two ways. Hoffman (1981) describes at length ways in which the patient's symptom is a reflection of the underlying problem in the family. Hoffman also describes work by Stanton and Schwartz which extends the mirror image to the situation in which a family becomes a 'special case' for a worker. The worker may then have to side with the family to protect them from the tendency of the organisation to treat them as an ordinary case, not requiring or deserving any special consideration. Rapidly, the relationship between the worker and her/his superior will come to replicate the relationship of the family and authority. We now see this as one example of a more general tendency for the helping professionals, whether or not they are working systemically, to reproduce in their work the problems of the family. For a general description of this kind of mirroring we do not feel we can better that offered by Furniss: 'Mirroring describes a process in which different members of a professional network take over roles in relationship to fellow professionals complementary to roles that different family members have in the family. The professional network enacts the family dynamics: for example, showing fragmentation processes and thus accepting the way the family sees itself, with certain members having specific roles . . . The professionals become bound in a non-therapeutic conflict-by-proxy which they are fighting for the family' (Furniss, 1983b, p. 214).

Mirroring can be a considerable obstruction to productive work. When a systemic team is having difficulties with a family, there is at least a possibility that they will mirror those aspects of the family that are responsible for the stuckness in family and team alike. They will then become incapacitated in much the same way as the family, and so be incapable of providing any solutions. However, we should bring positive connotation to bear here, and see how mirroring can be used to advantage. If mirroring reflects the processes by which a family has become stuck, then observing a team in which this is going on should offer clues to family processes that would otherwise be difficult to identify.

Exercise 7.2 (30 minutes)
Individually, make a list of five families or individuals with whom you have felt somewhat stuck. For each, write down two or three terms or brief phrases that describe important aspects of the way they functioned during your work with them. Take about 10 minutes for this.

Now go back to each case and consider whether each descriptor of the family also describes an aspect of how you felt and functioned in your interactions with them. Tick those for which the way of functioning that your term or phrase described for the clients was reflected in some way in your work with them.

In pairs, each offer one example in which your work mirrored the family process, and discuss whether thinking of your own functioning in this respect gives you a better insight into why the families were stuck.

Within family therapy, if the team is big enough, one or more members can be designated to observe the system of team plus therapist and comment on their processes. Even a lone therapist can decide to adopt a meta-position and try to take an objective look at their own behaviour as a clue to what might be happening in the family. In our own practice we have found that it is very useful, when we are feeling stuck, to step back and describe what the team is doing. Then we say: if that is what the family is doing as well, what does this tell us about why they are stuck?

Boundaries

A theme that runs through the uses of triangles (above) and geneograms (below) is the way that sub-groups (sub-systems really) are marked off by various sorts of boundaries. The concept is used particularly in structural family therapy, but any work which attempts to understand a system needs to be alert to the boundaries that are perceived by the participants. Within a family coalitions may most often be made on the basis of generation, but family of origin and gender are also common sources. The basis of a boundary may be either an attraction within the sub-system or as a protective border. Attraction may be that a group perceive themselves as similar: we are the good people in the family; we have fun; we have all inherited the Smith characteristics. Alternatively they may have a common objective – the adolescent chidren who want to attack parental rules, and therefore need to distance themselves from the younger children.

Boundaries as protective borders may be straightforward: parents who need to protect themselves from the demands of their children and vice-versa; a young nuclear family who do not want their lives dominated by grandparents. But sometimes boundaries are created to maintain secrets: a parent who is sexually abusing all of the children may create boundaries between them so that each thinks they are the only one with this relationship. In such cases each of the children may believe that they are protecting the others. A coalition between a parent and an older child who comes to adopt a parental role in the family also creates strong boundaries which exclude the other parents, and prevent the child from being properly involved with their siblings.

Once a therapist starts thinking in terms of boundaries, they can be an extremely useful punctuation of family processes. Some concentration on the idea is necessary because they are not always obvious, especially those that cross generational and gender boundaries. In one case grandmother, mother and daughter saw themselves as forming the core of the family, and had created such a strong alliance that all other members of the family seemed to circle round them helplessly. In another, the brother and sister who were seen as most like mother, were always expected to take father's side, while the other brother and sister (who resembled father) lined up with the mother. The family way of dealing with disputes was a kind of democratic process in which the people in dispute tried to recruit others to their point of view. This process reinforced the sub-system loyalty, creating a constant need to retain the 'vote' of each persons's sub-group. As a consequence, a boundary was set up so that alliances could not be formed between members of opposing groups. This process was stable because it invariably resulted in three people being on each side in any disagreement. The boundary was reinforced by perceptions of the other side being unreasonable, but the issues never had to be resolved.

Advanced Geneograms

Chapter 3 discussed the beginnings of a geneogram and showed how this can be used to give a visual representation of a family. We now want to extend this into how geneograms can become more informative by mapping information about a family on to them. We had also mentioned in Chapter 3 that a geneogram of the workplace or team can be illuminating and help to discover the roots and development, the myths and spirals in a working organisation. Also we want to introduce the geneogram as a therapeutic tool. Carter and McGoldrick (1989) have written extensively about the building and application of geneograms and provided splendid examples of intergenerational family geneograms including that of Freud's family.

Exercise 7.3 (20 minutes)

Constructing a personal geneogram
In pairs, return to the personal geneograms composed in Chapter 3. First, make sure that you have completed the geneogram to your satisfaction. Now, with help from your partner, consider where and how you began your geneogram. Is there space for older or new generations? What was easy and what was difficult in placing people in the geneogram? Is there any significance in beginning where you did?

May we remind you that geneograms are very powerful tools and need to be taken at each individual's pace. There may be exciting as well as painful moments of discoveries during this exercise and space needs to be made for this.

However, to continue, then you may move on to consider the quality of relationships: which are strong or weak, which stressful or antagonistic? What alliances, conflicts and boundaries exist? Having elicited these features, draw them in. It may now be apparent what themes, patterns, or secrets exist in the family. These may be further elicited by asking for stories about family members.

Finally, define who is in your family of origin, and in your family now, by drawing different coloured circles around those to be included.

When both partners have worked on their geneogram as far as they want to go, share similarities and opposites, and discuss in a group this format of learning.

Most families have a degree of complicatedness, so that a full geneogram can unravel a lot of complexity and allow patterns to be identified.

Exercise 7.4 (30 minutes)
Describe to a partner the composition of a complex family with whom you are working. Together construct a geneogram of this family. Notice how constructing the geneogram has added to your perception of the family dynamics.

Tools for Action

Geneograms

We will continue with geneograms for the moment, but in the form of therapeutic tools. We (and others) have found that a geneogram can be used very directly to bring about change in a family. If the process of constructing the geneogram is carried out with the family, all kinds of family perceptions can be clarified. Almost always there are aspects of the family that some members did not know about; sometimes facts that have been taken for granted turn out to be wrong; family myths can be challenged. Partly these effects come simply from an open sharing of information, but sometimes the ability of a geneogram to make relationships and timings very explicit has its own effects. Dates which do not add up, differing perceptions of the quality of relationships, missing relatives and so on are quite common.

Like any other powerful therapeutic tool, geneograms must be treated carefully, with respect for the clients, and with a willingness to recognise and deal with the consequences. Sometimes the information is not especially helpful, but may still cause upset. The commonest case, which some do find quite disturbing, is for children to discover they were born before their parents were married. It may be equally interesting to construct a geneogram of a team or mapping out 'family' relationships within an organisation or working team. Since working groups often develop family characteristics this can be an illuminating process. The information here would not be 'family-personal' but relate to work, career, where colleagues have worked before they joined a workplace, etc.

Before using geneograms as a therapeutic tool, you should get a colleague or therapist to take you through your own family geneogram. We have not offered this as an exercise because each individual should be completely free to choose with whom to do this. But do make sure you have this experience yourself before using it with families or individual clients.

A final practical point. We have found that the first session is too early for an exercise that results in as much exposure as can a geneogram. Wait until you have developed enough of a therapeutic relationship to withstand any feeling that the clients have let themselves in for rather more than they expected. Finally, it is important that the finished product is treated with respect. It can be kept from session to session and used as a source of ideas for a long time. In one family the daughter (in her twenties and very resentful of how she had been treated) insisted that she was ashamed of the geneogram, she screwed it up, and took it home to destroy it. Yet somehow it reappeared each session, battered but still legible, and her intense ambivalence towards it could be dealt with more constructively than her well practised rejecting responses to her parents.

Sculpting

The sculpt is a powerful tool in any situation since it usually exposes the ambivalences of the sculptor and makes clear the different ways in which family and sculptor perceive a situation within the family. Personal experience of a sculpt is important for the therapist and training is essential.

Sculpts can be perceived as circular (Walrond-Skinner, 1976) – the sculptor sculpting family members, the therapist supporting the task of sculpting and later commenting on the internal picture of the sculptor which has been made available for concrete (external) scrutiny. The sculptor arranges the family in the way they wish and during this process the therapist can assist them, particularly when the surfacing material becomes confusing to the sculptor or painful to any of the family. The term choreography has been used when describing a therapist who assists in a sculpt, though it is important that the representation is the sculptor's and not the therapist's.

Sculpting may be indicated particularly when therapy has reached an impasse or when a specific member has difficulties in verbalising what they wish to express. This may relate to a family who has difficulties in finding the words with which to express what they want to show, or when there are difficulties in the individual in reaching unconscious wishes, fears, or memories. A sculpt can help to express the differences between the inner world and what the sculptor thinks and how the rest of the family perceives this situation. The greater the difference between the internal image of the sculptor and how their sculpt is recognised by the other family members, the greater the impact and at times insight all of them can have. Heinl (1987) described this as: 'the greater the congruence between the reality of the "internal image" of family relationships and the constructed sculpt, the more the sculptor will be able to identify and recognise "meaningful" connections and the greater will be its emotional impact.' In a sculpt the positions the family members take up, their proximity, closeness and distance from others, the gestures they enact, the facial expressions they are given, all symbolise the family members' position in relation to each other.

Once the sculptor has found their position, the members all give feedback as to how they experience their position in the sculpt and how that fits in with their reality of the situation. This may then develop by asking members to move to a position where they feel more comfortable and noting both the changes, their effects, and who or what prevents them or holds them back. Thus, a sculpt can become a way of picturing the family's ideals or preferences about their relationships, thereby illuminating goals and the moves required to reach them.

Going One Down

A final example of a technique that creates leverage. This is the range of strategies that can be used to defuse expectations and to encourage the family to give a clear account rather than relying on assumptions. Therapists' one down statements ('maybe I'm not thinking clearly, could you . . .' or 'I'm still having trouble, just why is it a problem?' or 'I've got a rather concrete mind, can you give me an example') mean the family cannot use confusion as a strategy.

Tools for us

Zaphod: Don't go into that bar you might get drunk.
Arthur: What's wrong with getting drunk?
Zaphod: Ask a glass of water.

This joke, quoted from memory of *The Hitch-hiker's Guide to the Galaxy* by Douglas Adams, is naturally here with a serious purpose. It is to help make the point that therapists, as well as families, may become trapped in their assumptions and expectations, and to point to the liberating effect when limiting expectations are pointed out. The other reason for putting the joke here is that we think it is funny and that anything that helps you enjoy the book will help you get more out of it. More generally we believe that a family team has a duty to enjoy its work because only then will its clients benefit from its best energy and ideas. This section is about the needs of teams or people working on their own, and how to help them to do systemic work effectively.

We have continually stressed the importance of context, and one of the issues for teams is the context in which they work. Aspects of context are the role of the team in the organisation, the physical resources available, the operation of the team itself, and the kinds of relationship that it is appropriate to have with the families. Systemic teams are as affected by such influences as are families, and must take them seriously if they are to work effectively.

Family work is stressful and demanding, and it is not helped at all if it is being done against adverse circumstances. The contexts in which it is practised are extremely varied, so the solution will be different in each case. But as you establish a routine way of working, it is worth checking the following points. We have not suggested exercises because working contexts are so varied, but with each of the points those who work together, group, pair, or just individual, could consider the application to their work context, and then convene into larger groups to compare notes.

1) Could the environment be improved? Sometimes noises, smells, interruptions, flickering lights and so on are tolerated over long periods because someone else ought to be doing something about them. A meta-perspective may indicate that the gain in quality of life would far outweigh the cost if we took direct action.

2) Are potential problems such as sources of resentment within the team being tackled? We know of a team that solved a long-standing problem of some members always coming late by taking a decision not to worry about it. Being a systemic team does not create immunity to group processes, it just provides tools for dealing with them. But tools are no use if they are not used, and it is tempting to rush from one family to the next without attending to the needs of the team. Attending to the needs of the team is an essential requirement for long-term effective work.

3. Is the team being too successful? It is not just the unrealistic expectations that the team may develop. If the team is working alongside non-systemic colleagues, then there is a very real risk of envy. Such problems are best dealt with by open communication and consistent, honest, positive connotation of all of the work of the agency. But many teams encounter this as a very real problem, and it has to be tackled at the level of the organisation (see Chapter 9).

4) Does your management know (within reason) how you operate and why? Is there a reason to keep it a secret? If you think back to your first encounter with systemic family therapy you may remember finding at least some aspects rather bizarre or at least very different to what you then regarded as good practice. Perhaps you still do, but we hope that by now your perceptions will have changed. If you recognise a change it will be easier to see how management will need some clear messages in order to include your activities in their scheme of how things should be.

5) Are there techniques that would help us? A few years ago we started using an earbug. The team can send messages to the therapist without disrupting the flow of the session, and (rather to our surprise) therapists feel very supported by this innovation. Also the team behind the screen feel more involved in the minute-by-minute progress of the session. The earbug is our prize example of a new facility that has improved our work and our enjoyment of it. Maybe for you, double glazing the screen so you can discuss more freely, or reducing the time with the family so there is more time for team discussion, would be helpful.

6) Have we thought of everything we could do to make things worse? In many situations the strategy of working out in detail what you would have to do to make the situation worse can be informative.

Sometimes the list you come up with bears an uncanny resemblance to what you are already doing (the idea is usable with families as well). At least it will make explicit the actions that you need to avoid, and often it frees up thinking and makes it easier to suggest novel positive actions.

7) What is our problem? Why is it a problem? Who is it most a problem for? In what way is it a problem for them? If we did not have the problem what would we do differently? What is the minimum change that would make us feel it is not a problem?

Family teams are systems, and usually sub-systems of their organisations. They seem to work best when the principles of systemic working that have been developed for use with families are applied consistently to themselves.

Conclusion

You now have plenty of material with which to undertake this method of family therapy. Effective systemic work depends more on a consistent style and attitude than on any particular techniques, though using the techniques that others have found useful is one essential way of cultivating that style. It is beyond the scope of a book on its own to turn anyone into a competent practitioner, and we can see that the effect and meaning that this book takes on will depend on the context in which it is used. However one fundamental issue in developing your practice is the form and quality of supervision that you can arrange, and this is the final issue that we take up in this Section.

Chapter 8
Supervision

Supervision should not be regarded as a luxury in any sphere of professional activity, however experienced or 'senior' the personnel. It is beyond the scope of this book to make specific recommendations about the forms of supervision that workers should arrange. What we can and must do is stress that family therapy does produce a need for an outside view of what the therapist is doing. The techniques have the potential to be extremely powerful and so inevitably have a capacity for harm. In this chapter we review important aspects of systemic supervision, but it is a substantial topic raising many issues. A useful starting point for further reading is Liddle (1988) and other chapters in the same book.

Anyone can accept that supervision can be useful, but why should it be seen as essential?

(a) Why supervision? – dynamics within practitioners

Every practitioner approaches work with individuals, couples, families or groups with the effects of their own personal experiences. This inheritance of scripts will influence, not always in ways which are immediately apparent, a person's choice of profession and of interventions into practice situations. It can block their work and the change they are attempting to effect (Byng-Hall, 1988) because their experience of earlier relationships makes them susceptible to avoiding or 'failing to see' a particular focus, or to pursuing one 'favourite' hypothesis to the exclusion of other considerations. It becomes important for practitioners, therefore, if they are to be effective, to recognise the roles, scripts, patterns and myths to which they were exposed in their families of origin, the legacies bequeathed to them from these experiences, and their effects on their work and current personal situations. For instance, one worker became aware how, as a result of experiencing her own mother as failing to protect her, she was inclined to see mothers as abusive or neglectful, transferring her experience onto them and working with it there rather than owning her own pain. Another recognised that her struggle to see parents as potential perpetrators of abuse emanated from her experience of a close-knit family.

In other words, work with families can become blocked by the influence of workers' own scripts transferred from past to contemporary experience (Francis, 1988). This awareness is crucial if practitioners' actions or failure to act are not to be determined by personal material triggered by the abuse, rejection, hostility, coldness or indifference they encounter. This awareness also, in our experience, enables practitioners to retain and grasp the relevance of the theoretical models of family therapy to which they are exposed in learning situations. In our view, therefore, any training should include personal, experiential work.

Exercise 8.1 (20 minutes)
With a partner identify the key adults for you as a child. Identify the good and sad, happy and angry, caring and abusive (if any) experiences associated with each adult. In what ways have these experiences been carried over, either by repetition or determined attempts at correction, into your self-image, your current personal relationships, including child care, and your professional work?

(b) Why supervision? – the dynamics of the work
If the previous section alerted us to the phenomenon of worker transference, the carrying over of material from personal lives to professional work, here the focus is counter transference responses which are evoked by the work's complexity and emotional impact. Practitioners will encounter disturbed, violent and aggressive behaviour, intimidation and anger, or demoralisation and felt helplessness. The effect can be disturbing. The subject matter: physical injuries to children or sexual abuse; emotional relationships which rob children of innocence and warmth, acceptance and protection; this can swamp or enmesh practitioners in powerful emotions, making it difficult for them to sustain their professional role (Stevenson, 1986). The effect can be to leave workers feeling disgusted, intimidated or angry, rejected or vulnerable, demoralised or useless. These emotions, together with the high levels of anxiety and stress which can accompany working with families, can lead to organisations and individuals adopting defence mechanisms. Whilst designed for survival, these defences can create a closed system. Equally, practitioners may respond by becoming caught in symmetrical or complementary escalations. In the former, anger and hostility is met with anger and hostility, accounts are met with alternative explanations. The atmosphere is one of competitiveness. In the latter, the more clients are hostile, the more workers feel rejected or vulnerable. Here the position is one up/one down. For example, the more a family avoids a topic, the more therapists see confirmation in this of their own beliefs and pursue them regardless of any evidence which might indicate that their hypothesis is less than useful.

Individuals and families will also bring their own scripts. Their belief systems or punctuations on the problem and its 'causes', for example blaming one individual, will be clung to tenaciously. Attempts may well be made to recruit practitioners into these linear scripts. This is how some social workers come to be drawn into collusion with parents to 'ignore' abuse or to define it in a particular way, thereby becoming part of the problem and losing their ability, temporarily at least, to promote change.

Finally, when working with families, a considerable amount of material, verbal and non-verbal is elicited, complex and voluminous behaviour and dynamics observable. No one worker can possibly hope to see or respond to all this, let alone appreciate its potential relevance to pursuing or reformulating hypotheses.

Supervision, therefore, provides an opportunity to reflect on the impact of the work on practitioners and to manage this creatively. Put another way, it aims to enable practitioners to hold to their task and not be diverted by pressures from within themselves or from the family.

Exercise 8.2 (20 minutes)
When working with families/this family, what roles and tasks do you find particularly difficult or stressful? What might be contributing to these feelings? What defences have you adopted? What might enable you to hold more effectively to your task?

(c) Why supervision? – complexity of the work
In any therapeutic task workers will confront practice dilemmas. Taking the Steptoe family as an illustration, at what stage should Rachel's right to remain within her family give way to actions based on considerations of risk to her education and emotional development? How should considerations of Rachel as an individual be weighed against thoughts of her as a member of the family for whom she has an important function? What balance should be struck between the powers conveyed upon practitioners by law and the therapeutic knowledge gained from training? Who should decide what action to take in this case: therapists alone, therapists and family or therapists and magistrates? These practice dilemmas, more fully described elsewhere (Braye and Preston-Shoot 1990), entail role ambiguity: what is the task, who defines it, what is good-enough care? Definitions will vary depending who is asked and the position they occupy in the professional system. The dilemmas present very real tensions which practitioners must consider in each case.

There are no right answers. Without supervision, the opportunity to stand back, the chances of staying open and creative are greatly reduced. Rather, practitioners are more likely to engage in defensive or compulsive work, introjecting needs, injunctions and demands from elsewhere. With supervision, practitioners should be enabled to stay with the anxiety occasioned by the dilemmas, to consider and possibly convene the professional system to examine the place and roles of the various people in it. Supervision reduces the likelihood of refuge from the tensions being sought in dogmatic and rigid beliefs, and allows practitioners to consider what effects their interventions will have and on whom.

Exercise 8.3 (20 minutes)
Take a situation you are working with: what pressures are there on you to take a particular approach in this case? What tensions or practice dilemmas exist? From where do these pressures spring? How might you know if you are acting defensively or dogmatically? What next steps do you plan and why?

(d) Why supervision? – dynamics within teams
Professional systems, established to resolve problems, may by their activities and the complex dynamics into which they become drawn and entangled, maintain problems. Individual and collective defences may be employed to protect group cohesion and belief systems or to survive the impact of the task. We have explored in Chapter 7 concepts such as triangulation and mirroring whereby individuals and systems are co-opted into and unable to influence the family system. In mirroring, for instance, the family's dynamics and functioning is reproduced by the team/professional system into whom it has been projected and where it has remained because it hooks into (denied) vulnerability and conflict or into the potential for responsiveness there. Mirroring and triangulation, therefore, are information about the dynamics within the team/professional system and within the team-family system. They highlight the need for a system assessment besides a family assessment.

Exercise 8.4 (20 minutes)
Take a case known to you: what is your favourite hypothesis? What do you least want to see? What influences this? What would you feel and have to do if you found what you least want to see? What problems does this case pose? What positive reframes can you find for doing this work?

Exercise 8.5 (20 minutes)
Take a team or group of which you are a member. By circular questioning, draw out what it is like for members to be in this team, and in the professional systems of which they are a part in the cases they are working with. What positive reframes can be found for this involvement? What can they change in themselves, in the team and in the professional systems?

Types of Supervision

The most familiar form of supervision is reporting back. Its strengths are reflection and planning, managerial oversight to ensure the consistent implementation of policy, and consideration of the worker's professional needs to ensure an effective service. Its drawbacks stem from its lack of immediacy. Discussion follows some time after the events being related, substantial editing is possible such that the situation is not seen 'in the round' and the worker remains alone with the work. There is no immediate meta view, to disentangle the worker from difficult dynamics or direct attention to a particular focus.

The most familiar form of family therapy supervision is the one-way screen. However, such a facility is neither essential nor, indeed, necessarily the most immediate in terms of keying into and responding effectively to dynamics in the therapy room (Smith and Kingston, 1980). Each of the models considered below has advantages and drawbacks. Each requires preparation and review. Each provides a meta view to the therapy. It monitors how intention is translated into action. It formulates hypotheses. It observes the volume of communication in the therapy room which sheds light on relationships, and the impact of the therapist on the family and family on therapist. It provides a steady stream of encouragement, ideas and questions to the worker in the room. Each model provides a source of immediate, or fairly immediate learning, affording workers the opportunity to change their practice whilst 'in situ.'

Practitioners especially may feel distinctly apprehensive about some models of family therapy supervision. Indeed, having a supervisor in the room or team behind the screen can feel awesome, if not troubling. Work is 'on show', mistakes and uncertainties are visible. These anxieties can be projected onto families, in expressions such as 'they will not like it.' In our experience, workers and families 'forget' the supervisor or team after introductions to the method of working and personnel have been completed, permissions obtained and work begun. However, as part of the preparation for work, practitioners should acknowledge and discuss any fearful fantasies, simulate the models in training, and agree groundrules for operating the models.

(a) Live supervision
Here, the supervisor is in the room but outside the worker-family system and not directly involved in the interview (Kingston and Smith, 1983). This gives the supervisor an immediate feel for what is occurring in the session, an opportunity to view the process, including the part played by the practitioner, rather than be preoccupied additionally with content. The supervisor's interventions, by virtue of being given 'at the time', are forceful and affect the here-and-now. They provide immediate learning for the worker and suggest approaches which the worker-family system might wish to follow through. Since the roles of worker and supervisor are distinct, provided the groundrules are clearly agreed, this model should overcome the hesitancy and competitiveness which can occur in co-working (Smith and Kingston, 1980).

(b) One-way screen
Here, the supervisor/team communicates with the worker in the room by earbug, telephone, or knocking on the door. This arrangement allows team members to discuss actively what is occurring in the room and makes it more difficult for family members to attempt to subvert the process by by-passing the therapist and communicating directly with the supervisor. However, the whole team engaging with the worker can feel confusing and overwhelming. If there is more than one supervisor, we have found it useful to allocate roles: recording, observing, hypothesising and formulating interventions, communicating with the worker. This division of work can also be applied when formulating interventions in time-out: the worker engages with one supervisor whilst other team members observe and comment on the process between worker and supervisor.

The meta view to team functioning, sometimes provided by an outside consultant also, is especially valuable when the worker-supervisor system feels stuck. It has been developed by the Milan team so that they now consistently have a second 'observation' team sitting behind the therapy team throughout the session, and observing the system of therapy team plus therapist (Pirrotta and Cecchin, 1988). Of course an 'official' supervisor or consultant may at different times be in the observation team, the therapy team, or may be the therapist, depending on which aspect of the work they wanted to influence.

Exercise 8.6 (30 minutes)
Take the Steptoe family and role-play an interview using a hypothesis as formulated from Chapter 4. Arrange a team, either live or behind a screen. Allocate roles to the team: one a consultant to the worker on checking out hypotheses and keeping focus, one recording, one observing the family's response to the session, one identifying key relationships which might form the basis for an intervention or sculpt, one

looking for positive reframes of, and meanings for, the 'mess' (Reay, 1986). The role-play may be used to illustrate the value of supervision.

(c) Co-working
Initially as a team we used two therapists in the room, in addition to a team/supervisor. Co-therapists are sometimes also used without additional supervision, especially by social workers. Several arguments are advanced in favour of co-work (Dowling, 1979; Preston-Shoot, 1987). In training co-working allows a student to be paired with a more experienced colleague. Two therapists allows the modelling of a collaborative relationship and permits division of the work into task and process monitoring functions. When one worker feels stuck or overwhelmed by the size, demands and nature of the family, two workers may be seen as appropriate (Piggin and Watson, 1979).

However, the advantages may be overstated. Without a consultant outside the therapist-family system, there is no guarantee that co-workers will be any more successful in avoiding enmeshment in the powerful dynamics which sessions may elicit. This is because both workers are inevitably engaged in both content and process, however the work is divided. Thus without supervision, it does not follow that two workers will necessarily be any more effective than one in working with particular families. As a training modality, co-working may be unnecessarily complicated. The student may not feel sufficiently confident, in themselves or their co-worker, to venture contributions. Alternatively, they may hide behind their more experienced colleague. Without thorough preparation, neither student nor the family will benefit from the hesitancy, uncertainty and awkwardness felt in the session. Moreover, if roles are unclear, or experienced as difficult, muddle and competitiveness may be what is modelled. In our experience, the security which co-working appears to offer may be illusory. Careful preparation is essential of the co-work relationship and thorough planning of how sessions will be approached. How the family interacts with the two workers must be monitored, to see if the workers are mirroring problems within the family (Coulshed and Abdullah-Zadeh, 1983) such as being split into hopeless and optimistic positions or hard and soft roles.

Keeping the Supervision System Open

The supervisory system, like any system, can become closed, either because it actively colludes with the family in avoiding particular areas or because of its own scripts or because it is hooked into mirroring dynamics projected from the family system. However, various strategies will help to keep this system open. First, each worker over time will develop their 'internal supervisor' (Casement, 1985) whereby they continually ask themselves what is happening, to them and in the session, and what roles they are being asked to play. This curiosity and looking for the not so obvious will give each worker a perspective on the system, and their role within it, from outside. Secondly, the team should swop roles, both to increase learning and to avoid each member becoming trapped in any one role (Reay, 1986).

We have already indicated the value of ascribing a definite role to each team member and of using a consultant as someone meta to the team process with a family, even if this person is a team member who takes other roles on other occasions. Our final prescription for positive practice in keeping the supervisory system open is review. This provides for feedback into the system. Thus:

1) What sort of team member do I want to be and am I allowed to be?
2) What are my resources, skills, qualities and knowledge?
3) What, if anything, gets in the way of me being the team member I want to be and using my skills, resources and knowledge?
4) What am I most anxious/unsure about in terms of (a) my role, (b) the team, (c) working with families? What might others in the team be anxious/unsure about in terms of their role, me, or family therapy? How is the work affecting me? What difficulties does the work present for me and the team? How do we respond to these difficulties?
5) What I like/dislike about the team is . . .
6) What I can do about my dislikes is . . .

Preliminaries

Before any supervisory system can become fully operative, various preparatory considerations are necessary. Equally, whenever there is a change in team membership, the preliminaries should be repeated. Finally, periodic reviews should focus on the developing experience of the team. The objective is to ensure that the system remains open.

(a) Having the basics for coming together

In Chapter 10 we list some characteristics of open systems. Crucially important here is a willingness to work with differences, theoretical agreement on the models and methods to be used, clarity of roles, and different skills and strengths brought to the tasks. These qualities are essential for effective co-working and teamwork. They may be explored through discussion and exercises such as sentence completion (Preston-Shoot, 1987).

(b) Operational culture

This concerns the ethos of the team. For example, we have found it useful to do enjoyable things together, both regularly and after difficult sessions, in order to unwind healthily and to encounter each other in situations other than work. Coming together with a variety of role tags (gender, professional titles, training qualifications, levels of experience, status and roles in other settings) requires that status and position be (re)negotiated within the group. Equally, a culture which accepts the right to say no to work or to particular roles, and the inevitability of not knowing sometimes will enable team members to express uncertainty and retain realistic degrees of therapeutic ambition.

(c) Agree the Groundrules

The first groundrule to establish is whether supervision is concerned with consultation or monitoring and management; that is, whether the supervisor/team is responsible to an agency for ensuring that organisational procedures are implemented. Even where supervision is more akin to consultation, help of a professional kind in responding to the demands of the work, the principle that the therapist is in control of the process should be owned and messages from the team should be framed in such a way that distinguishes when suggestions carry more of the force of strong recommendations or instructions (Kingston and Smith, 1983). The second groundrule to clarify is the way the supervisor/team will operate during a session. Interventions to the therapist should ideally be brief and clear, neither too frequent to interrupt the therapist's train of thought and approach nor too seldom to risk leaving the therapist feeling unsupported or stuck. Interventions may take the form of praise, encouragement or support to 'stay with it' to the therapist, or suggestions about how to question around a hypothesis or move forward from an apparent stuck position, or actual messages to the family. Longer messages or discussion when stuck should take place in time-out.

The third principle to resolve is how decisions are made: who decides when the team should intervene; how are decisions about what interventions to deliver reached (that is, how the team handles this process); what roles will team members take in respect of the session when the therapist is in the room or with the team for consultation?

When students are being trained in a team, these groundrules should be reviewed and clarified, alongside induction into the team's model and style of work and theory of change. Moreover, issues of status and power should be specifically addressed since, not uncommonly, students feel that they lack both and yet are asked to participate fully in the team's work and process. Team members must consider, therefore, how to enable such participation.

Supervisory Questions

Supervision, whether of the worker-family system or the worker-family-team system, should address key questions which are designed to keep the system open; generate information to formulate or revise hypotheses; focus on the interconnectedness of meaning, behaviour, and patterns within the system; and inform the interventions given to the system's members. These key questions include:

1) What are the central issues?
2) What is the problem?
3) What is happening (now)?

4) What for?
5) Why now?
6) What roles are we being allowed/invited to play?
7) How do the family see and react to the worker? How does the worker see and react to the family? How are therapist and family working together?
8) What is the plan for the session/meeting? What are people wanting to achieve? What might be interfering with this?

Exercise 8.7 (30 minutes)
Simulate a session with the Steptoe family, using a supervisor/team and observers to the team plus family system. The observers and supervisor/team members should practise formulating interventions: what interventions would they make, when and why; what might be the effect of these? These interventions may also be given. In addition, the supervisor/team should apply the key questions in order to analyse the process of the 'session' and the observers should focus similarly on the process of the supervisor/team. After the simulation exercise, the whole process can be reviewed in terms of what facilitated and what hindered work with the family.

Section 2
Specialist Issues

Now that you have established and practised the basic techniques of this model of family therapy, we can move on to examine a few crucial areas in some depth. Over the last decade systems therapists have found that their expertise has application well beyond families, and even within families their role is not always comfortably described as therapy. Wynne, McDaniel and Weber (1987) have discussed the implications of this trend in some detail, and suggest that it would be much more accurate to describe people working in this way as systems consultants. However these authors recognise that such a title would not necessarily create appropriate expectations nor, rather more concretely, jobs, and so they suggest 'family consultant' as a compromise.

In Section 2, as we extend our discussion to wider systems, it becomes more realistic to talk of consultation rather than therapy and we will adopt this convention. After discussion of extensions to a wider variety of systems, we take child abuse as one of the most common, most serious, and most problematic arenas for the application of systemic family therapy. Finally we review some of the exciting ideas about theory and practice that have emerged in recent years, and then deal with the crucial issue of how we evaluate what we are doing.

Chapter 9
Beyond the Clinical Setting

Family therapy models are sometimes thought to be applicable only to clinical settings. However, family therapy is alive and well in various contexts, such as in voluntary agencies, social services, day hospitals and inpatient adolescent units (Miller and Cook, 1981; Treacher and Carpenter, 1984; Campbell and Draper, 1985), and as a framework for approaches to management (Palmer and McCaughan, 1988). We have used a systemic framework in a variety of contexts:

1) With families in their homes, with a live supervisor whose role is introduced to the family as being there to help the therapist and the family. Team consultations take place in another room or outside in the car.
2) With social workers who feel stuck in their work with families or professional systems, especially using geneograms and hypothesising to unravel the interactions.
3) With parents whose children have been hospitalised, focusing on the interactions between and among parents, children and ward staff.
4) With staff in residential settings, focusing on sub-systems, boundaries and triangles between staff, residents and outside agencies.

We are not just staking a claim here for this model's versatility. Context determines meaning and should inform practice. Actions undertaken in one context will have a different meaning and effect if reproduced in a new setting. Something that works in one setting may become absurd or offensive if persisted with in another context. Thus, new contexts will hopefully inspire useful variations in technique and understanding rather than the reproduction of, potentially, redundant solutions. The original ideas will emerge enriched by new associations.

Nonetheless hard-pressed practitioners appear wary of theory, deterred by the jargon in which therapeutic approaches are couched, and unconvinced of their applicability to the harsh realities of life in their settings. Thus, the challenge exists to overcome the objections and demonstrate the relevance of taking family therapy approaches out 'onto the streets.' In this chapter we will seek to show how systemic thinking can be adapted for use in non-clinic settings, both as a framework for understanding and thinking, and as an intervention technique. Then we will consider some of the objections and show how they are better viewed as challenges to be more inventive.

Objections as Sources of Further Ideas

One assumption is that the model is inapplicable to statutory work, that the statutory role cannot be integrated with other therapeutic roles. However, keeping them separate distorts the reality experienced by clients, namely that there is both a statutory order and problems to be resolved (Dimmock and Dungworth, 1985; Currie, Evans and Oliver, 1988). Further, it creates an unhelpful split between 'good' and 'bad' workers. Thus, whilst it remains true that a statutory order does define one individual as 'the problem', this does not preclude involving other family members or systems in exploring the nature of the difficulties, nor does it invalidate such concepts as neutrality.

A parallel assumption is that the approach is only applicable in clinics where the therapist's role is assumed to be unambiguous and monothematic (therapy only). However, clinic therapists are not necessarily free from the influence of other roles and responsibilities. Family therapists often see families where abuse has occurred. They may be required to assess prospects for rehabilitation or asked to submit reports to courts where decisions relating to the welfare of chidren are debated and resolved. This decision-making role about the future involves several roles which have to be negotiated explicitly (Bentovim and Gilmour, 1981).

It is not impossible to hold the roles together, to work therapeutically whilst exercising statutory powers. A first step is to acknowledge statutory responsibilities, the duties and limitations these impose, and the circumstances in which legal obligations would be invoked. This marks out the non-negotiable aspects of the role. The next is to explore the extent to which service-users see themselves as clients and the images they hold of the setting to which they have come or been referred. Compulsion to attend may prove demotivating unless users accept the existence of difficulties and the method of work designed to tackle these. Settings may evoke images, for example of 'the welfare', somewhat removed from the therapeutic aspirations of workers. Such a clash in perspective, if left unexplored, may sabotage the work.

Significant others in the wider family and/or worker systems add to the complexity. Their goals may differ from the worker's. Their co-operation must be secured and, where necessary, their permissions regarding the intervention plan. To achieve this, the system can be brought together to work these clarifications into a working agreement. This avoids covert double-agendas and spells out the exact nature and purpose of the work. It relates the worker-user encounter directly to the network and systems which underpin it. It acknowledges statutory orders, where these exist, but moves beyond the linear punctuation which they represent by engaging the network and wider systems in problem clarification and solving (Dungworth, 1988).

We have already discussed the Milan concept of neutrality. This concerns not the therapist's state of mind but the overall impact of their activity on the family. It is widely seen as inapplicable because it is assumed to mean non-involvement and non-confrontation (Treacher,

1986). However, this is a misrepresentation. Clearly, if required to act according to legal duties, workers are in a different position and cannot maintain neutrality in the strict sense used here (Cecchin, 1987). Neutrality means challenging everything, siding with no-one, resisting linear punctuations of cause and effect and moral judgements, and avoiding coalitions (Selvini Palazzoli, Boscolo, Cecchin and Prata, 1980a; Hoffman, 1981; Cecchin, 1987; Burnham and Harris, 1988). Thus, in letters, interviews and telephone calls, the aim is to challenge without taking sides. In interviews, for instance, if individuals dispute a view taken by professionals, neutrality suggests that workers do not engage in a battle over who is right but enquire what the individual thinks needs to happen for others not be concerned (Mason, 1986). This offers the possibility of introducing new information or perspectives into the system. Neutrality does not mean the absence of strong opinions or abdicating responsibility but rather curiosity into alternatives. For example, it directs workers to challenge and explore gender assumptions underlying the way families organise their roles. It does not mean condoning everything but remaining open and creative by moving around the system from the perspective of those involved, including the worker. Thus, even when working according to legal duties, the concept of neutrality directs workers to retaining curiosity rather than simply accepting linear morality.

Concretely this can mean taking an attitude towards a macho man like: 'we see that it is very important to you to see yourself as a strong person within this family, someone that others, such as your partner, can depend on. Also, you have seen other strong men, maybe in your family or friendships, having their comforts looked after by the women around them. Accepting that this is what you are used to and that change does not happen overnight, can we work out how your partner can develop her capabilities outside the home and you extend yours by bringing them into the household tasks.' If neutrality is lost, workers are liable to accept simple explanations of badness and madness, or to transfer one blame game (the family's: its all that person's fault) for another (the worker's: it's all your responsibility) (Walrond-Skinner, 1976). Substituting one battle over definitions for another, in this way, is unlikely to result in effective problem-solving.

Criticisms also centre around power and gender. In relation to power, critics point out that not all people in a system have equal power but that systemic thinking assumes they have. Access to employment, physical power, finance, gender, age, class, culture or education all shape the degrees of power and influence which people may exert in a system. Thus, not all members of the Steptoe family have equal power, although readers may disagree on who, in what contexts, is most/least powerful. So, just as it would be a nonsense to assume equal power and influence, and to deny the existence of conflict or oppression, either within the family or between it and wider systems, we have to ask how members of the system have become and remain fixed in one position, and to find ways of incorporating and working on social and political levels alongside the interpersonal in hypotheses and interventions.

Critics also argue that systems thinking has ignored gender and embraced the dominant model of the family (Hare-Mustin, 1987). However, family therapists are beginning to address the paternalistic organisation of society, and to challenge family members' assumptions about their relationships (Piłalis and Anderton, 1986; Williams and Watson, 1988). An essential requirement for would-be therapists, therefore, is to examine their own values, scripts and attitudes on power and gender. Otherwise, they may not be able to see and challenge structural inequalities, confront the abuse of power and enable people to question how they use it, or empower individuals in their relationships to reach for the changes which they desire.

A common complaint is that systems theory is essentially conservative. We believe rather that the theory has been used conservatively and that theories are only as good as the people who use them. The reasons for this have been explored elsewhere (Preston-Shoot and Agass, 1990) but include the mandate to professionals from society and therapists' enmeshment in dominant social constructions and values which are difficult to shake off.

Another objection is that health and welfare agencies are not, nor in the current political climate allowed to be, systems orientated (Adams and Hill, 1983). There are four elements to this. First, much welfare work obtains its mandate from a combination of an ethical duty of care to clients (Stevenson, 1988) and the law (Blom-Cooper, 1988). Whilst the former perspective may direct practitioners to the wider system of which individuals and families are a part and by which they are influenced, the latter mainly provides legal authority only to intervene in the lives of individuals and families (Kingston, 1979) and not the public and social ills which create or exacerbate individual difficulties. Thus the law, a creation of dominant groups, reflects an individual treatment model. Secondly, this feeds into a dominant view of causation and solutions as linear. Pathology is located in the individual or family. Social and economic inequalities and their effects are glossed over. Institutions like families, schools and courts, promote dominate values and cultural norms. Change at political and social levels is restricted. Accordingly, it is difficult for agencies and workers to challenge effectively the dominant social constructions of, say, gender roles, family life, race and age, and how for individuals and families such views limit the range of behaviours and solutions available to them.

Thirdly, there are various orientations available to inform the structure and philosophy of service delivery (Whittington, 1977). The current vogue emphasises economics over effectiveness; rules, organisational procedures and control of the 'deviant' over users' definitions of their problems and needs. Practitioners may find their professional assessments of need compromised by managers and politicians who plead lack of resources.

Fourthly, there is the nature of the work. Society offers welfare practitioners contradictory or ambiguous messages, for example about the rights of parents as against the risks to and rights of children in child protection work (Stratton, Davies and Browne, 1988). This is leading practitioners and agencies to abandon therapeutic work and professionally assessed risk taking for safe work and defensive practice (Harris, 1987).

However, these four elements all point to the necessity of employing a systems perspective. Change is not as simple nor as rational as linear models might suggest. Individuals and families in the present carry the legacies of past scripts and experiences which may result in their being rigid and stuck, unable to adjust and evolve, or chaotic and without any stability. Individuals and families exist in dynamic relationship and interaction with a wider context such that a focus exclusively on therapeutic work with individuals and families, to the exclusion of their material needs and experiences of and interaction with economic, social and political systems, will prove incomplete and inadequate. Finally, the relationship between the law and professional practice frequently poses dilemmas and conflicts. An ethical duty of care and a legal mandate often appear as polarities, posing awkward tensions: when to intervene, where and how; on whose decision; for what purpose (Braye and Preston-Shoot, 1990). Thus, problem-maintaining cycles may easily become established within families, between agencies or between families and agencies. Systems frequently collide. A perspective on this is essential if practitioners are to work effectively and for change.

Some Applications

The model outlined in this book directs practitioners to:

1) 'helping solutions' can become part of the problem;
2) symptoms or behaviours, rather than being the cause of difficulties, can be attempted solutions;
3) behaviour, therefore, when seen in context, has a meaning or function. It may, for instance, be the best adaptation which seemed available to avoid interpersonal or intrapsychic conflict or anxiety;
4) the need, therefore, to focus on transactions and to include everyone in the system in order to promote change on the basis of a clear appreciation of what is happening.

These principles, as a framework for understanding and as guidelines for action, may be applied to various parts of the 'helping encounter'.

(i) Referrals: Workers in the helping professions are trained to be helpful and caring. This produces comfortable images: something is being done because something clearly must be done. It brings order to chaos. However, how effective is it? For example, referrals of children 'beyond control' are often accompanied with either a request that they be taken into care or with an injunction to 'change them, not us'. Practitioners who automatically agree to the first request not uncom-

monly find their efforts rewarded with a request for the child to be returned home. Responding to the injunction to focus on the child merely maintains the problem because it ignores interactions. In this scenario, practitioners are incorporated into the system's way of going on being. They must not be too successful otherwise the conflicts and stresses, the dynamics which are 'covered' by the problem, will be unmasked.

At the referral point, it is useful to consider the various referral games (Preston-Shoot and Agass, 1990) which can be played out, and to restate the problem in interactional and systems terms. Thus, in this system . . . or in this family . . . or for this individual . . . Setting out a formulation in this way will uncover the 'because' clauses (Reder, 1988): what is the context? What maintains the behaviour (intrapsychic anxieties, interpersonal dynamics and/or interaction between the individual/family and social/economic systems)? What is happening? What makes the system function in this way? What is the problem? Such a formulation should direct practitioners to possible interventions.

(ii) Family-agency interaction: Most agencies hold cases where other professionals express considerable concern, frequently demand that 'something must be done' and where exhaustive interventions have failed to produce change. Surrounding one family (two parents and five children) was a considerable professional network: two social workers, educational psychologists, police, health visitor, teachers from two schools, day nursery staff, home helps and family aides. The four oldest children were 'home on trial', care orders having been made because of neglect. There were sharply differing views in the professional network, the teachers especially holding very negative views about the parents, concerned at what they regarded as a lack of progress on the children's hygiene, behaviour, lack of stimulation and on the condition of the house. The social workers were more positive, seeing progress in the parents' attitudes since the care orders were made. The professional system rarely met. There was no agreed plan. Two contracts between social workers and the family had 'failed'. The house remained chaotic and the children dirty and under-nourished. The social workers felt expected to do something and the team leader instructed them to negotiate a 'better' third contract, that is to try harder. In group supervision, however, it was suggested that attempted solutions, together with pressures and communication from the professional system, had become part of the problem. The family's view had been neglected. It was unclear what the parents saw as objectives for change. The social workers had become triangulated and enmeshed in the family-professional network system. With previous interventions having 'failed', a difference rather than more of the same was required. The supervision group suggested that a network meeting be convened to discuss perspectives and concerns; to resolve what change was being sought, by whom and why; and to involve the family in determining what change was to be attempted. Various working agreements

between the family and members of the professional network might then be possible.

The involvement of wider systems and a team or network's processes can affect task clarity. How individual practitioners function is not solely due to their resources, skills or knowledge. Whether the work is effective is not necessarily the responsibility of the individual or family being worked with. Systems sometimes collide. Perspectives, values, positions in the network, and procedures clash, as when teachers and social workers blame each other for continuing difficulties with a child, engaging in an unhelpful battle over the correct view to be taken in the case. Systems sometimes also enter into collusion, either by denying the existence of problems or their part in maintaining or exacerbating them, or by detouring conflict away from difficult areas by focusing on safer issues, or by not coming together to discuss their involvement in cases, as in the above example. Thus, systems may contribute to problem formation and maintenance. Agencies may become locked in blame games centred on 'whose fault is it?' Whether or not excluded from decision-making about the work, families can become trapped in agency and inter-agency dysfunction.

Again, key questions are useful for understanding and for formulating an effective intervention which will unlock stuck sequences. Thus (Dimmock and Dungworth, 1983; Dungworth and Reimers, 1984):

1) In which system is the problem?
2) Why are we involved?
3) What is expected of us?
4) What function are we being asked to carry out? What role is being pressed on us and why? Is this appropriate for us to undertake?
5) Do we need to clarify our functions and, if so, with whom?
6) What are the rules governing this system and the interactions within it?
7) How do people view the interactions, the intervention, their position in the system and the position of the other participants?
8) Do the family feel that they have a problem? Is this the problem the agencies are working on or is the problem the way the agencies are involving themselves and each other with the family?
9) What do people, including the family, believe that the work is concerned with and that others are concerned about?

These questions take people to a meta position. The questions enable them to consider their own involvement but also the perspectives held by others involved.

(iii) Family-worker interaction: The model we have presented in this book is an appropriate model for all settings. This stems from two beliefs. First, that the model encourages purposeful planning and direction in the work, by focusing on clarity of assessment and linking interventions directly to that formulation. Secondly, that linear causality, centred on

blame, is less likely to promote change than positive reframing of people's intentions and tasks or prescriptions that offer the possibility of introducing difference into the structures and belief systems through which people organise and negotiate the demands of their lives. Thus, battles to establish 'the one reality' are unhelpful. When serving a place of safety order, a social worker avoided the entrenched and escalating positions which follow from presenting the reasons for the decisions, finding them being disputed, and each side becoming more convinced of their own perspective. Rather, the social worker positively connoted the parents' anger as concern and suggested that they might consider what they could do so that members of the case conference, which took the decision, did not have to feel so concerned.

In all forms of work it is essential that workers consider the context of the work, the inter-relationships of those involved, and the influence of other systems past and present, both in seeking to understand the difficulties and in determining an appropriate intervention. Workers cannot make change happen. They can, however, seek to co-evolve an understanding with those involved. After all, rather than being 'bad', the adolescent may find the local peer group a powerful influence, or be deeply troubled by conflictual relationships at home, or be depressed by difficulties in finding employment. The current experiences of foster parents may be linked with their own experiences of being parented as children. These may be linked with the scripts and needs which they have brought into their commitment to fostering. The older person may have become the scapegoat for avoided conflicts in the extended family.

Exercise 9.1 (30 minutes)
Take the concepts introduced in this book. Write down how your work would be different if you applied them. How would you practise differently? What would be the implications of working in this way for you and for your agency?

Preconditions or More Tools for Us

Since, as we have already pointed out, this model presents a way of working which challenges what we might term orthodox thought in welfare agencies, it is unwise to introduce it without preparation. Consequently, family therapists who have sought to apply the systemic approach to their own agencies have highlighted the importance of describing the model to managers, outlining in non-jargonistic language its implications for the agency and seeking permissions; forming support groups to provide consultancy; considering how the model might contribute to agency procedures and policies, and to other workers' experiences and skills (Dungworth, 1988). Specifically, we would offer the following practice guidelines:

1) Go slowly and do not rush in.
2) Do not try too hard but allow ideas to percolate.
3) Be modest in ambition, limiting self-expectations, and beginning with less complicated situations.
4) Find positive reframes for present practice. Agencies and practitioners are more likely to consider difference if they feel their present work is not diminished or dismissed.

Chapter 10

Close Encounters in and Between Professional Systems

As family therapy has become established, practitioners have discovered that solutions might sometimes be found more easily through the professional systems with which the families were involved. As work with professional systems has developed, practitioners have discovered that the techniques and concepts that had been devised for work with families were highly effective when applied to a range of other systems. This is not too surprising since both families and organisations are systems made up of the same kinds of people. Many of the characteristics of families listed in Chapter 2 also apply to organisations, so it might be expected that the methods of hypothesising and intervening would also be effective.

If there are similarities between family and organisational systems, there are also certain differences which mean that not all family therapy techniques can be applied directly in other contexts. The problems arise, again as might be expected, because organisations operate within a different context from families. Family therapy is oriented to the development of individuals through their family relationships, and a rather different emphasis is required in the techniques before they can be applied to helping organisations achieve their objectives. Nonetheless, one theme in this book has been how to construct stories to illuminate how the various components of a system connect and inter-relate. Techniques such as geneograms, sculpts and circular questions, and concepts such as mirroring, boundaries and scripts, have relevance here in understanding processes and intervening effectively in professional systems.

One of the fundamental differences is that families are primarily concerned with relationships, while organisations are primarily concerned with their task. Sometimes families may give tasks a higher priority than relationships, and then they are in trouble. Sacrificing the family to the career of one member is an obvious example.

From the other side, organisations may become so concerned with relationships that they lose sight of their objectives. There is an old joke of a company report that included the statement 'productivity has risen 50% and morale 90% since we abandoned the policy of being one big happy family'. All systems must find an appropriate balance between the needs of the members and the external objectives. If a system becomes locked into an overriding concern with tasks or relationships, its energy will become locked away with the result that, although self-contained and in equilibrium, it will tend towards stagnation and disorder. It will become a closed system, fixed and unable to adapt its goals and structures to changes in context and environment (Evans, 1976).

Paul Watzlawick, in his Foreword to *The Hidden Games of Organisations* (Selvini Palazzoli, Anolli, Pisano, Ricci, Sacchi and Ugazio, 1987) points to a fundamental aspect of families that is shared with organisations. A system may hold together in such a way that its outward functioning is stable, but at the cost of internal disorder. Many systems, organisations as well as families, manage to tolerate the internal disorder and so remain operative. However, in some the cost is that one or more individuals become physically ill or psychologically disturbed. As the disturbed form of functioning becomes established in the perceptions and expectations of all involved, the system comes to rely on it for its stability. In our framework for understanding things, we have here a linear punctuation that reverses the primary direction of causality. The system will construe its discomfort as being caused by the pathology of the individuals, and will find justification for blaming the individuals especially if their solutions have become somewhat redundant. A more useful and historically meaningful account would indicate that the pathology derives from the individuals' attempts to adapt to the system.

Exercise 10.1 (10 minutes)
Think of a colleague with whom you have recently discussed the workings of your organisation. Now write down some examples of times when they complained about the effects that the characteristics of an individual or sub-group were having on the organisation. Now write down some ways that those characteristics might be seen as adaptations to the demands of the organisation.

Note how far the redirecting of causality opens up possibilities for change.

Like families, organisations have an existing structure, and a history from which the present form of operating is derived. This predates the intervention of the systemic consultant. In this sense, as Selvini Palazzoli, Anolli, Pisano, Ricci, Sacchi and Ugazio (1987) point out, both are different from groups which the group therapist or researcher sets up from a collection of individuals so that they can observe the processes by which they form themselves into a group. The first difference arises because the consultant usually has much less control over the initial processes by which they join the system. This is particularly true if the consultant joins by becoming an employee of the organisation, but it can also derive from a brief to interfere only with one part of the organisation's functioning, or to do nothing that would upset certain aspects of present functioning (don't annoy the union/the boss), or to maintain a myth about the consultant's own organisation. In Chapter 5 we went to some lengths to indicate how important it is to maintain control over the preliminary phases of interaction with a family, and not to lose manoeuvrability by accepting preconditions. In work with organisations there may be no alternative to relinquishing this freedom.

Like families, organisations and professional systems must adapt both in response to their members' development and growth, and to changes in the external environment. For instance, social services departments will have to consider the implications for their structures and goals of government policies about care in the community. Similarly, the type of supervision required by a newly qualified practitioner, or the role of a manager in a newly formed team, must be reviewed as the practitioner gains experience and the team develops. Like families, however, organisational systems may experience difficulty in being open and responsive to change, in adapting to difference internally or in the external environment. Indeed, the potential of helping systems to become part of the problem is well established and, when working with individuals and families, and/or within professional systems, it is unwise to ignore this possibility.

Exercise 10.2 (15 minutes)
Consider the team to which you belong. When did it last review its structure and work? Are its structures appropriate or have the demands of the external environment or the development of its members created the need for review and change? Who in the team is most likely to agree/disagree with you?

Systemic Concepts Adapted for Organisations

As with families, systemic concepts can illuminate encounters in and between professional systems.

1) *Boundaries and Communication*: Inquiries into the deaths of or serious injuries to children regularly highlight deficiencies in intra and inter-agency co-operation and communication. Professional systems and organisations, like families, may be divided into smaller sub-systems, some of which hold executive authority and decision-making powers. If boundaries between the sub-systems are too loose, who holds decision-

making authority and how it will be used will be unclear, as will who should be exchanging information with whom and about what. Chaos will be a potential feature here, with professionals meeting only rarely. If the system is too rigid, as in some hierarchical organisations, communications may not reach their destination and the inflow/outflow of information between the sub-systems, and between the organisation and its environment, will be severely restricted.

Alternatively, what is being communicated may either be unclear or place the recipient of the communication in a bind. In child abuse there is no consensus about when discipline or family structures become physical or emotional abuse, nor what constitutes unacceptable risk to children at home, except at the extreme end of the abuse continuum. The balance between parents' and children's rights is defined differently at different times and by different people. There are no right answers. Yet practitioners are required to protect children and not to fail or make mistakes. Here communication and expectations are at times contradictory, at times ambiguous.

Exercise 10.3 (20 minutes)
Draw a geneogram of a team you belong to and the organisation of which it is a part. How clear are the boundaries? Are they rigid, loose or flexible? Do they allow or restrict the flow of information? How clear is decision-making authority and where does it reside?

Geneograms provide clarity about who relates to whom, who communicates with whom, and the type of communication. They illustrate whether boundaries are permeable or rigid, clear or blurred, and whether professionals are enmeshed, as if one, or disengaged, or whether relationships and boundaries allow informational exchange within the system and between it and other systems. Geneograms have much to say about whether relationships are conflictual or harmonious, passive or active, one-way or two. As such, they may identify processes such as triangulation, enmeshment or scapegoating.

2) *Punctuation and Scripts*: In Chapter 1 we illustrated how people respond or adapt to the context as they perceive it. We demonstrated that there is no one reality but that, because they can only see their punctuation easily, people in a system are apt to pressurise others into seeing things from their point of view. Accepting individuality or difference, without blame or judgement, which might enrich understanding, gives way to battles over what is really happening and what really should be done. As in families, members of professional systems will have their individual punctuations, built up from values, training, experience, and roles.

Exercise 10.4 (20 minutes)
A professionals' meeting: Gardener family.
Two years ago Jane (age 14) disclosed to a teacher that her father, Fred (age 41) had been sexually abusing her over the previous three years. Her mother had left the family home six years ago when she developed a relationship with another man with whom she is still living in another part of the country and by whom she has two more children. Following disclosure Fred was interviewed by the police. After some initial denial, he admitted the abuse, pleaded guilty and received a prison sentence. Elizabeth (age 9) and John (age 7) denied any abuse and there was no medical evidence to suggest they had been abused.

After the disclosure Elizabeth and John were placed with foster parents and Jane went to an assessment centre. Although at one time it was hoped she would join her siblings, the foster mother felt unable to take Jane after she had absconded from the assessment centre several times and taken an overdose. Jane was placed in a children's home and although initially there had been a stormy time, she had settled and begun to relate increasingly to the care staff, especially the officer in charge.

Fred has now been released from prison on parole. He is living within the neighbourhood in lodgings arranged by his probation officer. He has asked for access and rehabilitation into the family. Social services has convened the professionals' meeting to determine a response to this request. This is the task of the simulation exercise to be chaired by the senior social worker. Cameo roles for each participant are given at the end of the chapter but otherwise they are asked to develop their own attitudes, especially in relation to the beliefs which influence their contributions to the meeting, their feelings about their position in the system, and the decision they believe the meeting should reach. Observers are asked to note how processes which occur during the meeting unfold.

---

*After the exercise, take feedback from the observers and participants, concluding with the senior social worker. The feedback should aim to elicit the following material for discussion:

1) Was the objective of the meeting achieved? If yes, what facilitated or hindered this? If no, what processes sabotaged the task?
2) To what extent were participants able to see beyond their own punctuations?
3) What signs of closure were evident in the meeting and where were these emanating from: anxieties about the case and its possible implications; different models and belief systems about sexual

abuse or child care practice; stereotypes of each other; defensive practice; in whom the power of decision-making finally resides, leaving some people feeling powerless?

4) What themes and alliances were evident? What observations may be made about the communication and meta-communication which took place?

In all probability the perspectives held by the participants in this meeting will have resulted in considerable disagreement regarding appropriate courses of action. Additionally, labels on the theme of madness or badness may have been attributed by some to others on the basis of their contribution. As this exercise reveals (together with the example in Chapter 9 of another professional system's interaction around a family) different roles, values and perspectives will lead different professionals to see and present different things. Whether collision or co-operation results depends on the extent to which participants can embrace punctuations other than their own and consider how components of the system fit together.

3) *Secrets and Myths*: We described in Chapter 2 how family functioning can be affected by myths and secrets which are designed to prevent feared calamities. Thus, family members may present images of a close-knit unit, to themselves and others, in order to keep hidden feelings which they believe might threaten relationships.

Professional systems are also likely to contain myths and secrets. The most powerful secret in social work, for instance, which of course everyone knows about but does not talk about, is that tragedy is inevitable in child care/child protection work. The myth is that correct assessments, if such as possible, and training can offset the depths and intricacies of human personalities and prevent serious abuse. The 'solution' is to try harder to prevent tragedy. The myth and secret are rarely confronted openly, either because of the additional anxiety this would expose practitioners to, or because it would challenge one motivation for working in this field, namely to protect and help people, or because of anxiety about how others might then view the future of social work.

Exercise 10.5 (20 minutes)
In your team and its interactions with wider professional systems, what strengths and themes, alliances and exclusions, communication patterns, scripts and secrets do you observe? What is their meaning or function? How do members experience membership of this team? What do members believe would happen if this information was shared, especially outside the team? What does this suggest about the system?

---

4) *More of the same*: In Chapter 9 we gave a case situation where social workers attempted to negotiate 'better' contracts with a family in response to the breakdown of previous agreements. As in families, professional systems can sometimes become locked into one solution which is reproduced in 'bigger and better' versions. What we must understand here is what makes it difficult to abandon the 'solution'.

Exercise 10.6 (20 minutes)
Consider the case described in Chapter 9 and hypothesise about what made it difficult for the professional system to abandon the 'solution' of re-negotiating contracts. Then, take a case with which you have been struggling for some time. List all the things you have done to try and solve it. Are all your solutions just 'more of the same'?

---

5) *No weakness; No shocks*: In Chapter 2 we illustrated how the power of expectations in families can produce these two tendencies in patterns of family interaction. They may also be found in professional systems. Just as individuals may feel that they have no alternative than to act in ways determined by the family, so professional systems may believe that they must act in ways prescribed by society.

It has been well documented that organisations, and individuals within them, incorporate into their behaviour and structures defence mechanisms designed to avoid doubt, anxiety, practice dilemmas or uncertainty occasioned by the work (Jaques, 1955; Menzies, 1970; Braye and Preston-Shoot, 1990). Equally, the more professional systems are exposed to the emotional and physical demands of the work, reflected in the inevitability of risk in decision-making, increasing demands and static or diminishing resources, volume and complexity of work, the more likely practitioners are to seek to minimise error, risk and exposure by defensive practice (Harris, 1987).

This defensiveness reveals itself in organisational structures: office arrangements which distance workers from service-users; moral terminology, for example about undeserving clients; procedures on which the myth of infallibility is constructed; ideologies of need which, currently, elevate economics above professionally assessed needs; and ritual task performance to eliminate decisions.

It may be seen also in the behaviour of individuals. Among the more familiar signs are:

1) Directiveness and authoritarianism: statutory and agency authority are emphasised, the expression of feelings is avoided.
2) Safety first: everything is investigated; weekly contact but often without clear purpose.

3) Distance: users placed into categories; presenting problems only are worked with to prevent workers from feeling overwhelmed by demands.
4) Deflection: the authority role is avoided.
5) Projection: clients are seen as hostile, unmotivated or manipulative, to enable workers to retain acceptable self-concepts.
6) Arrogance and 'as if' omnipotence: a denial of the emotional effects of the work: 'as if' certainly revealed in dogmatic assertions such as children never lie (about sexual abuse) rather than children have a right to be believed (cf. Williams, 1966; Mattinson and Sinclair, 1979; Addison, 1982; Preston-Shoot and Agass, 1990).

The systemic concepts of 'no weakness' and 'no shocks' shed some light on these processes. Society exerts a powerful influence on practitioners' behaviour. The expectation is that professionals will 'solve' or tidy away the troubling thoughts and images, the inequalities, and the disadvantages present within society. Professions like social work, therefore, are established to provide a protective script (Preston-Shoot and Agass, 1990). Conflict between family members, or between them and society or some professionals, is detoured and avoided by referral to a third party who is, thereby, triangulated. What is wished for is the avoidance of conflict and anxiety rather than change. This is reflected in referral games, where professionals can become embroiled and entangled in unclear or inflated expectations and lose their leverage to influence systems and achieve change (Carl and Jurkovic, 1983). It may be seen also in the reactions which follow calamities, such as child murder, which the behaviour of professionals was expected to prevent.

Under pressure from outside or from anxieties and feelings evoked by the work, professional systems may engage in a symmetrical escalation known as groupthink (Blackler and Shimmin, 1984). Here one hypothesis is pursued and evidence about alternatives disregarded. Conformity is emphasised. This may create a feeling of group security but the system's ability to perform its tasks effectively will be reduced given the absence of critical appraisal or reflection.

Alternatively, the same pressures from families or other systems may result in professional systems spiralling into overactivity: the more that is expected, the more the professional system assumes sole responsibility for the problem, their efforts matched by increasing expectations and inactivity, if not passive hostility, from the families or wider systems who are the focus of their efforts or the source of their mandate for intervention. Another possibility is that the more professionals feel pressurised to act, the more paralysed, drained, exhausted or useless they feel. Either way, we have circular patterns of interaction where the component parts reinforce each other.

Finally, the professional system may take on and act out the needs, conflicts and feelings which have been denied by family or societal systems, thereby mirroring. For example, secrets in a family may be paralleled by non-communication between professionals; roles, such as laissez-faire versus firm control, taken by family members, may find echoes in discussions between members of a case conference.

All these processes provide potential clues to underlying individual, family or societal dynamics. The systems approach to understanding and intervening in them, to avoiding muddled thinking and confused practice, centres on five tactics, all of which are designed to enable practitioners to assume and retain a meta position.

1 *Hypothesising*: Forming hypotheses enables you to achieve a meta perspective about process and patterns, themes and differences, about issues and where they may be enacted. Hypotheses, which are essentially stories about a system, enable you to clarify in which part of a system problems may lie and, therefore, where and what interventions may be appropriate. The key questions will be familiar by now: what is happening; why is it happening now; what is the meaning, function or purpose for what is taking place?

2) *Bring the system together*: This enables workers to see how the whole system interacts: the position individuals and agencies adopt, the relationships and interaction patterns, and the contributions each makes to the maintenance or resolution of problems. It enables feelings to be shared which might otherwise frustrate progress. Sharing everyone's perspectives together helpfully defines the problem and clarifies underlying dynamics, suggesting possible interventions. It avoids enmeshment in one person's definition, or the projection of problems onto one individual, or detouring responsibility for solutions onto one 'omnipotent' saviour allowing the rest of the system to remain unchallenged. Convening the system reduces the likelihood of acting out disagreements or of splitting into 'good' and 'bad'. It engages everyone in the change process, clarifying why people are involved; for what purpose; what they expect in terms of change; and what they will contribute towards achieving the desired situation (Dungworth and Reimers, 1984; Pottle, 1984; Coulshed and Abdullah-Zadeh, 1985; Corden and Preston-Shoot, 1987).

3 *Going meta to oneself*: This entails applying a supervisory viewpoint to oneself (Casement, 1985) and one's own position in the professional system. There are two elements to this. In relation to teams and professional systems, each person's experience of the present context is seen through filters which may to some extent distort current perceptions. Byng-Hall (1988) has described clearly how a family script evolves over generations and influences contemporary work and perceptions. Significant teams in the past will contribute to present punctuations and influence, in some way, one's interactions. Thus, what images do I hold of teams and of other professionals? From where do these images emanate? What teams have I belonged to before? What

have they given me? What did my family and professional training give me in relation to professionals, teams and teamworking? How does this affect my present experience and work?

In relation to the task, another set of circular questions may prove helpful:

1) What am I most anxious about in terms of (a) my role, (b) the task, (c) those others involved?
2) What might those others involved be most anxious about in terms of (a) my role, (b) the task, (c) their role?
3) In what ways is this affecting the task?
4) What am I here for? What am I not here for? What do others think I am/am not here for? What are they here for? What might others expect of me? How can I positively connote if I cannot provide this? What is my role? What do I/others feel about this? What roles do other people have? What do I/they feel about this? In what ways might this affect the task?
5) What do I know, think and feel about the task? What might others know, think and feel about the task (skills, practice wisdom, theories and method, experience)? In what ways am I able/unable to use these attributes? If unable, in what ways and how can I change things in me/in the professional system?
6) How is the work affecting me? What difficulties (personal triggers, professional dilemmas and problems) does the task present for me? Who knows about this? What difficulties might it present for others involved? What can I change in me/in the professional system? What positive reframes can I find for what is in me/in the professional system?

4) *Going meta to the professional system*: Each member of the professional system will bring personal and professional issues and anxieties in relation to the task and teamworking. The key question, therefore, becomes what does each person bring? The questions listed above may provide helpful answers but further clarification can be obtained by exploring stereotypes, fantasies and beliefs about each other's professional groups; anxieties about and approaches to the task; assumptions about roles. Differences and uncertainties should be explored (Holdaway, 1986) since otherwise they will frustrate communication and co-operation. Equally important, is clarity about what professionals can/cannot do, for instance in terms of statutory powers and duties, since people often labour under false assumptions that professionals have greater legal, that is controlling, powers than is the case. Elucidating the constraints under which people work: legal, policy, resources, and describing functions held by each professional should reduce the potential for misunderstanding (Dimmock and Dungworth, 1983).

5) *The Task*: Having considered the process of the system, the task must also be addressed if the system is to remain open rather than feel threatened and act defensively. Within this focus there are four components. The first is creating the setting: explaining the approach, clarifying where power and authority lie and under what circumstances it may be used, stating the legal position. The purpose and overarching goal for the meeting must be agreed and sub-goals teased out where appropriate. Where goals differ, work may still be possible within the difference if participants can agree to work co-operatively to achieve their respective aims (Corden and Preston-Shoot, 1987). As with families (Chapter 3), scene setting should also include what people are hoping for from the meeting and consideration of what will happen if the meeting is unable to provide this (Reder, 1986).

The second component surrounds who identifies the problem. Is there consensus on what the problem is, or that the problem is a problem and not an over-reaction to ordinary life-cycle events (Coulshed and Abdullah-Zadeh, 1985)? If consensus is absent, who agrees/disagrees and what does this indicate about the family, task and professional system? How is the problem a problem for each member of the professional system, and why worry? This clarifies belief and value systems, for example about appropriate work to take on or good-enough child care, together with statutory obligations or exposure to pressure. Put another way, this is another 'what is the problem?' sequence (Chapter 4).

Thirdly, what problems could the problem create or what has happened to the workers in the workers-plus-family system? Here professional systems can beneficially focus on factors in the situation which professionals might be sucked into and mirror or act out, or on possible reasons for their 'stuckness'. These dynamics might originate in families, professionals acting out the roles of family members (Street, 1981), or in society's expectations about the task, reflected in angry exchanges about rights vs risks, care vs control, what we feel and do if users refuse help. This focus alerts the professional system to factors which might make for non-rational decision-making: pressures from outside wider systems, from the family, from within. How, then, does each member view their task, the task of others, each member of the family?

The final component surrounds decision-making. What decisions are possible and what non-negotiable? What changes are sought and why: worker anxiety, client interest or . . .? What change would people settle for? Of all the possible decisions, which are least acceptable? Eliminating possible solutions in this way will leave meetings with the one decision about which the system feels least anxious (O'Brian and Bruggen, 1985).

Exercise 10.7 (45 minutes)
Re-convene the professionals' meeting on the Gardener family (Exer-

cise 10.4). First, those not selected to play the roles should hypothesise, to formulate a meta view on this system. Thus: what hypotheses would you formulate about this system? What circular questions would you use to test out these hypotheses? How would you portray their relationships in a geneogram or sculpt? How might this differ from their perspective? What positive connotations can you find for their position in the system?

Now, with one person acting as a systems consultant, with others as a team, re-run the meeting. Then, consider the same questions when taking feedback as are listed after Exercise 10.4. On this occasion, however, focus also on whether, and if so how, the presence of the consultant made a difference.

Invariably, the presence of the systems consultant is helpful in enabling people to move beyond their own view, examine inter-relationships and consider other perspectives. This is hardly surprising. It is exceedingly difficult, though often expected of workers, to focus simultaneously on task and process, to be both part of the system and meta to it (Coulshed and Abdullah-Zadeh, 1985). The meta position or supervisory viewpoint provided by a consultant is enhanced by neutrality. The consultant avoids agreements and disagreements with members of the system, remains beyond any blame game or attempt to find fault and, hopefully, is not dragged down and in by the difficult dynamics of the task. Rather, the consultant encourages curiosity (Cecchin, 1987), looking beyond the clash of linear punctuations and misperceptions of what others do, to appreciation of the system from all sides and the positions of the people in it. This stance, and the circular questioning prompted by it, introduces new information. This enables the system to evolve, to move beyond tightly constructed and defensive personal and organisational scripts to being open and creative.

In conclusion, the invitation is to curiosity, to hypothesising: looking for what is not so obvious and to what may be happening, feared or avoided. The invitation is to a meta perspective, to prevent the system from closing down.

Gardener Family: Professional System Roles

Probation Officer: you met Fred just prior to his discharge from prison. You can see that he is genuinely fond of his children, acknowledges he was guilty of the abuse, which after all happened after his wife had left and he was bringing up the children single-handedly. You feel that Fred has paid the cost socially expected and are keen to optimise his rehabilitation.

Social Worker: you inherited the case from another worker after the investigation and trial had been completed. With the care staff you have been through some of Jane's ups and downs and see her as a very likeable girl. You are aware of your primary responsibility to protect all three children. You see abuse primarily as an (male) abuse of power and are sceptical about the prospects of rehabilitation.

Senior Social Worker: you have recently been promoted and become involved in this case. You are aware that 'care' does not completely fill children's needs and you have heard that sometimes families can be rehabilitated. However, you are also familiar with the adverse publicity of cases in other areas that went wrong.

Officer in charge: you have struggled through the bad patches with Jane and are keen to maintain the more recent improvement. You have at times found it difficult to appreciate that Jane misses her father and worries about him, whereas her angry moods have been more understandable. You would like the chance to continue work with her and feel you have something to offer her.

Foster Parent: although distressed at first Elizabeth and John have settled well and are now well integrated into your family. You know the story and have seen how the abuse affected Jane and would not wish to see anything like that happen to Elizabeth. You have never met father but believe men like that should never be trusted again.

Chapter 11

A Systems View of Child Abuse

Working with families when child abuse has occurred is one of the most difficult areas, though if therapy has helped the family change to a non-abuse style of parenting, the process can be one of the most rewarding. We have successfully worked with families who have physically abused their children, who have emotionally abused them and when children have been failing to thrive for non-organic reasons. Working with families and tackling the specific issues of child sexual abuse has attracted much attention during the last decade in the U.K. and a systemic way of working has been found useful in many cases. We will discuss the issues related to the different forms of abuse and how they might be understood using a systemic perspective. What can be said emphatically at this point is that all forms of child abuse must be seen in the context of a multidisciplinary and multi-agency framework and a systemic way of working facilitates this.

Generally we think of child abuse as a linear and causal relationship between a caretaker and child, and the interventions are usually directed towards the abused and abusers. However, tools like 'going meta', 'neutrality' and 'circularity' (to mention just a few) have been found to be relevant when approaching treatment of these families. Positive connotations are probably the only tool which cannot be applied readily around the issue of the abuse itself, though it may be used about other areas of functioning and dysfunctioning in the family. Attempting a positive connotation about the abuse may be useful for team discussions, however, to free the team to think of alternative ways of looking at the situation.

James and MacKinnon (1990) have given a thoughtful account of their concerns about systemic practice. They argue that in cases of sexual abuse the issue of responsibiity is not addressed, and that '. . . the family therapy literature concerning incest fails to perceive the patriarchal context of abusive behaviour and consequently blames the victim' (p71). Family therapists must recognise that positive connotations must be handled with great sensitivity. The abuse of children cannot be positively connoted. But, as we pointed out in Chapter 1, positive connotation is not about claiming that the behaviour at the end of the chain is positive. It is an honest attempt to understand how each of the people concerned, over the course of time, became trapped into this pattern of behaviour. In the case of child abuse, a full description of all of the interlocking spirals, which go back through the childhood of the perpetrator and probably to preceding generations, is not usually possible. But we would claim that the stance positive connotation provides is still immensely valuable in several aspects of abuse work. If the task is to decide whether the perpetrator will abuse again, then we need an alternative to dismissing them as evil or crazy. However difficult, we have to try to see how they came to the behaviour. Once this understanding is obtained, at least in outline, some judgement about what will need to be different to prevent abuse in the future can be made. Perhaps the answer will be total separation of the perpetrator from the family, perhaps it will be a change in the understanding that the parents have of the needs of children and the roles of parenting.

When child abuse occurs in a family it is not helpful to perceive the abuse as between one adult and one child only. It has to be perceived as being part of the overall functioning of the family. Furthermore, the systemic practitioner has to take different systems and their interactions into account: the wider systems and networks associated with the family either in their neighbourhood or the professional systems that may make an input. We have discussed such thinking and conceptualising throughout this book and will here concentrate on how this relates to abuse in particular. Families do not live in isolation but are connected closely or distantly to an extended family and a neighbourhood, including schools, general practitioners, child health clinics, work.

Systemic thinking has built up a store of knowledge which enables the practitioner to consider the patterns of dysfunction in a family when child abuse has occurred. Though a linear causal relationship exists, when for instance a parent hits a child, this does not help us to come to grips with the complexity of the situation. It does not answer the question why the incident might have occurred, leave alone how best to intervene.

Hanks and Stratton (1988) discuss the power relations and coalitions within families. They point out that many families find ways to balance off influence and power, resembling something like equivalent leverage. However, men particularly have an unequal share of power within society. Parents and men in families can easily use excessive power. Under duress this power can become oppressive and be used to abuse. Forming a coalition in abusing families may take the form of recruiting one of the children as an ally against the other parent which can either lead to a breakdown in boundaries and possibly to an inappropriately close relationship with one parent, or the child can become a 'scapegoat', acting like a 'distance regulator' between the parents and producing behaviour which invariably leads one of the parents to an angry, possibly violent outburst. The distance regulating model and spiralling of such events are described in Chapter 7 and in the failure to thrive example in this chapter. These give an idea of the outcome in such cases for the child and family.

When stress is building up between the parents the child may create a diversion by attracting attention. This then disrupts the frightening process of the adults' destructive interaction. Over time the child has to engage in more and more disturbing behaviour in order to continue having the effect, but by this stage the frustration and anger of the adult/parent is vented on the child for his/her 'naughtiness'.

One issue must, however, be made very clear: though concepts like neutrality have been found to be helpful, the abuse, whether physical, emotional, or sexual, of children inside and outside the family must always be the adult's responsibility. There can be no substitute for that. Neutrality is not always possible for the family therapist who is also called to court to give evidence. Decisions need to be made at such points. However, a systemic approach can afford the flexibility to construct interventions, to side with one party (the child) and at the same time recognise that the abusive interactions somehow maintained the system in its dysfunctional mode. Summit's (1983) paper on the accommodation syndrome made very clear what the position for the child is. Being able to view child abuse from a meta and systemic position has, in our experience, freed us from having to withdraw from families, rather than in any way condone the abuse.

Physical Abuse and Failure to Thrive

While a systemic model would attempt to understand the physical assault on a child in terms of adaptations and transactions (see Chapter 2) and clarify the role the child has within that model, this still means that responsibility for the abuse remains with the abuser. A systemic view would recognise that the abused child in such a bind is completely helpless and will have to make whatever adaptations they can to minimise the short-term damage. Often this will inevitably take the form of doing more of the same rather than being able to find a solution out of this complex situation.

Marie and Paul came to family therapy because Leann and Bill were both failing to thrive. Leann had been hospitalised with an infection for the third time during recent months and Bill was also struggling to keep his weight along the third centile. He had become a lethargic child.

Looking at the geneogram we see that both parents had been married before and that there are a number of children. Not all the children lived with Marie and Paul but Carl, Jane and John did. Kate and Jenny lived with their mother but visited regularly at weekends. The relationship between Marie and Paul had deteriorated and neither had an amicable relationship with their ex-spouses. There were constant battles between the adults and consequently a great deal of tension in the house. At one time it had looked as if Marie and Paul's marriage was going to fail, but Leann had become ill and Bill lost a lot of weight. This united the parents and both worked hard to care for the children but with a minimum of contact between the parents. Because

Marie's ex-husband had applied for custody of his/their two children the tension had grown even more and Social Services and a Court Welfare Officer had become involved in the family. A Health Visitor came weekly in connection with Leann. A Paediatrician and the family's general practitioner played an active part in the management of the family.

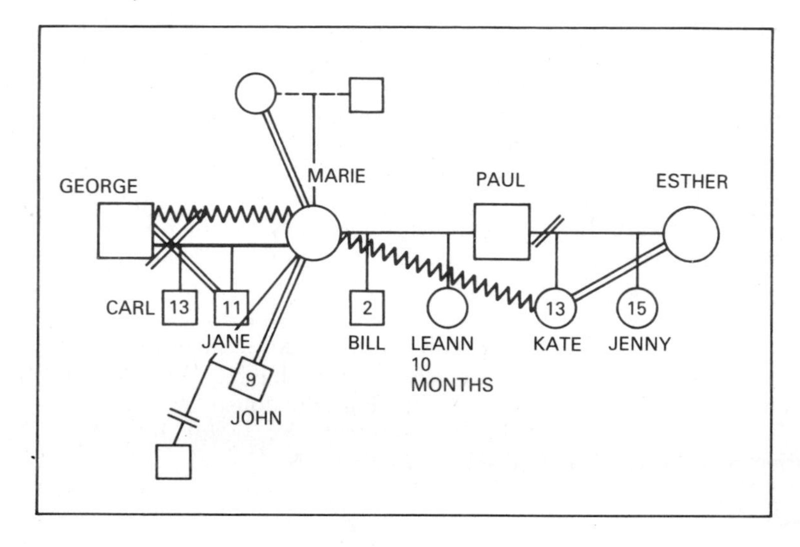

Figure 11.1 Case Study

The school had recently become concerned for John who was behaving in a disruptive way, apparently for no reason. Marie's parents, who had been critical of Paul, came to help out at times but always expressed their view that George had been a much better father and that Marie did not cope with Bill and Leann because Paul was 'just no good'. Recently, Paul had hit Marie, Leann had to be taken to the local casuality department because she had a burn on her hand and a case conference had put the child's name on thc register. No coherent story as to how this had happened could be established. Both parents denied that they had caused the injury to Leann. Marie and Paul had been very appreciative of the work the social worker did with them and felt supported. At the recent hospital admission of Leann the couple had been close, though their relationship had deteriorated again after Leann returned home. Bill and Leann continued failing to thrive and a referral for family therapy was made.

As we plotted the geneogram in preparation for a professionals' meeting the number of professionals involved became clear. We mapped on the friends and family members that were also involved and we recognised a rich pattern which could potentially be fertile ground for good advice and/or disagreement over how to help this family to manage.

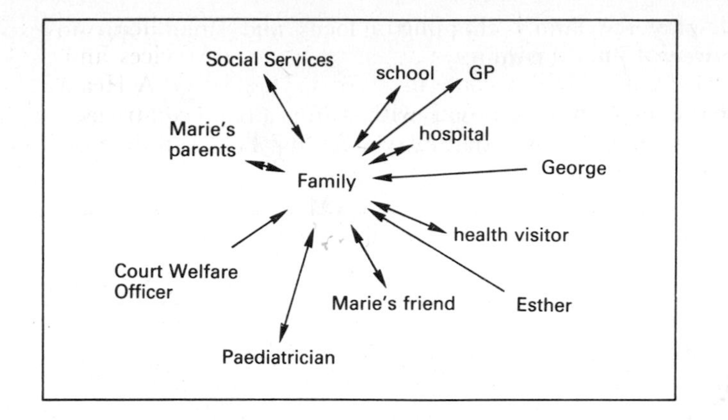

Figure 11.2

It is always informative to create a geneogram of the professionals and other systems known to be involved in a family. It clarifies who to invite to a professionals' meeting and what can possibly happen if crucial members of these systems decline to participate in the planning for the family. It also confirms the hypothesis made above that there is a rich pattern of different people involved and this may create as well as alleviate tensions.

What is also known is that child abusing families in particular seem to have considerable powers in engaging professional systems and holding on to them or replacing agencies or workers in an attempt to get or sabotage help.

This is quite a different approach from looking at why the parents may have children who fail to thrive, or what is wrong with these children and how we can remove the symptom. We can now begin to describe the interactional patterns that may contribute to the family dysfunction and hypothesise about the maintaining factors in this family.

One hypothesis must be that the function of the children's failure to thrive was to keep the couple together and yet distant, each occupied and focusing attention on the children rather than themselves or each other. This keeps the marriage afloat. The children 'helped' and stayed thin. When the children put on weight because of the interventions by the professionals, the failure to thrive may either be replaced with another symptom or another child takes on the role of distance regulating and becomes the symptom bearer. We know that John is already 'standing by' so to speak, with creating problems at school.

Exercise 11.1 (90 minutes)
Create the geneogram adding in the information you have gained from this description. (10 minutes)

Role-play the family choosing a focus and small topic to explore (between 15 to 30 minutes)

Role-play a family therapy team meeting planning the professionals' meeting. Decide who to invite and what the focus of the meeting should be (10-15 minutes)

Role-play the professionals' meeting (30 minutes).

---

*REMEMBER to de-role after each exercise.

In this family the function of the symptom, the failure to thrive, was to keep the couple united in the care of their children, and the marriage afloat. This family was seen over a considerable number of sessions. Professionals had become increasingly more anxious over the children's failure to thrive, at times more anxious than the family. The family recruited many helpful workers and individuals who would eventually get locked into a position of replacing the parents, taking on their responsibilities, and attempt to solve the family's problems single handed. This would lead to enmeshment and loss of neutrality and eventually be reproduced by a mirroring in the professional system of the family dynamics. This might include giving the couple contradictory advice; de-skilling other professionals; and telling the family that they did not have a problem at all, just thin children who were stubborn and would not eat. The spiralling pattern of such interactions is described in Chapter 7.

Issues Raised by Sexual Abuse

Sexual abuse may, if anything, be more destructive than other abuse. It has short and long term effects, difficult to remedy. Much has been written about the management of families where sexual abuse has occurred and we refer the reader to Glaser and Frosh (1988) and Bentovim, Elton, Hildebrand, Tranter and Vizard (1988) who rightly point out that '. . . treatment of sexually abused children has to be multifaceted. We would not regard family work alone as sufficient to meet all the needs evinced by various family members' (p182). The child or children may need treatment on their own or in groups, the parents may need treatment on their own or in groups. There may be a most beneficial outcome to work with the non-abusing parent and child or with a sibling group.

We have been most successful when working with:

1) *Parents and children when the abuser was outside the family*: Family therapy may help a family cope with the discovery that one of the children in their family has been sexually abused. The child may be in individual therapy or in a children's group at the same time. What families have said has helped them most when coming for therapy

together, is that they were able to see each other's position in an environment where they felt supported, where their actions were often understood, and where they were helped to look at what they might have done in the past differently. Concepts like neutrality, meta position, double binds, and circularity are useful tools to explore the family's fears and concerns. Parents blamed themselves for what had happened and became stuck in their thinking for the future. For many of them it was difficult to see how they could protect their children, or teach them how to stand up to adults that made them uncomfortable, leave alone abuse them, while at the same time remain respectful and able to co-operate in positive events. The family, as it were, took on the victim behaviour as a whole and found it impossible to move on in life. If children had developed sexualized behaviours out of the abuse, parents often were at a loss what to do. Should they ignore it and hope it would go away? Should they chastise the child? Some blamed the child and felt that if they had told the child once not to engage in sexualized behaviours the child should be able to comply. Family therapy provides us with an alternative understanding of aspects of abuse. It does not have to contradict or undermine other perspectives but can be used to generate alternative ideas for action and future plans.

Exercise 11.2 (45 minutes)
Role-play a family, mother, father and two to four children, discussing in a family therapy session that they do not know which way to turn, how to behave towards the abused child in particular, how to understand him/her, and what they are supposed to do with him/her when s/he becomes sad, cannot sleep, will not play with other children and, what is most important to the parents, what to do when s/he behaves in a sexualized way. They are wondering also how to tell the grandparents that a cousin (in his late twenties) had sexually abused one of the children.

De-role and discuss.

---

2) *Remaining parent seeking help with children after the abusing parent has left home*: Situations arise and the remaining parent needs help with how to cope with the children and brings her/his own agenda, like 'how could I have prevented it'. Often parents feel defeated by the process of having to care for sexually abused children and consequently become unable to look forward. Instead they remain stuck with the issues of the abuse, rather than being able to develop new ways of coping. As mentioned above a systemic framework may provide one way of working for a solution for the family.

3) *Foster and adoptive parents*: Foster and adoptive parents have a particularly difficult task, not only of accepting a child into their family, but accepting a child with possible sexual behaviours which appear challenging and unacceptable. These parents often take on the blame if they have not succeeded in 'remoulding' the child. More seriously they may become involved in patterns of interaction with the child which can become very negative and set up a spiral which demoralises family and child alike.

These families have to work with professionals and their networks. They may also have to accommodate the original family, not only in their thinking, but also in actual practical planning (access visits, parents visiting the child in the foster family's home, supporting the natural non-abusing parent in their attempts to build a relationship with the child while in care). The foster parents at times become the ones who 'supervise' access. They also have to deal with a child that makes further disclosures once s/he feels safe.

The foster parents may also have to work with the fact that the children attend for therapy. They may feel that this process will not help the child 'forget' the abuse and settle down. This may cause conflict in the way they conceptualise the care of the child.

A systemic approach has in our experience helped foster and adoptive parents make transitions which would otherwise have been difficult. The tools discussed in this book can be applied in such cases. The families will each have a unique profile and the tools will have to be used accordingly.

Exercise 11.3 (45 minutes)
Role-play foster father and mother, foster child, social worker and therapist. The foster mother is very concerned about the child's sexualized behaviour, someone had suggested to the foster parents that they could do nothing about it and should most certainly not intervene. The child was like that because s/he had been sexually abused and the foster parents had begun to believe that, therefore, all they could try and do was to understand that this is how it was and that this child could not learn how to do things differently or give up some of the behaviours.

Using tools from previous chapters, role-play a session with a family therapist and team.

De-role and discuss.

---

4) *Sibling groups:* Brothers and sisters who have been taken into care because of sexual abuse share the same family myths, beliefs and assumptions. The biggest issue for the children in such groups relates

to the fact that the abuse of each of them may have been completely hidden from the others, until one of them disclosed, and all of them were taken into care. Circular questioning may show each of them what the others think without 'putting each other on the spot'. Very often one child or all the siblings had allowed the sexual abuse of themselves because they believed that this would protect the others. Uncovering this is a delicate process and again neutrality of the therapist, circular questioning, considering the situation the children are living in systemic terms, and testing out hypotheses are all ways in which the children's relationship with each other may be explored.

Recognising who is closest to whom, or just how distant they have been from each other, discovering each other's strengths and weaknesses and addressing the competition which invariably exists between siblings are some of the major tasks for this group.

Exercise 11.4 (45 minutes)
Form into groups of between two and four children with one therapist. Take up roles. Now discuss why one of you made a disclosure at school. In this case the medical revealed that all the children had physical signs. However the four have not heard each other acknowledge that each of them had been sexually abused by their father. Do not discuss the details of the abuse. Find out whether or not each of the children had been abused. Use the tools and identify which ones have been most helpful.

De-role and discuss.

Conclusion

Child abuse and neglect confront everyone who is concerned with families with the most intractable problems. In this chapter we have tried to indicate how our work with families in which abuse has occurred has been helped by a systemic orientation. Child abuse, particularly sexual abuse, does pose strong challenges to whatever approach is being used. Our view is that for those actually working with abused children and their families, a systemic mode of working is sufficiently flexible to be of great value and can be extremely helpful in at least some areas. To conclude we want to emphasise our awareness that there are immense problems at all levels of this work, and that systemic methods are just one tool to be harnessed in our struggle to cope with a long-standing epidemic of which we are only just beginning to appreciate the magnitude.

Chapter 12

Extending the Effectiveness of Systemic Family Therapy

The approach to family therapy described in this book is a continually developing set of techniques and ways of understanding, and if you look out for relevant publications you will find a rich source of new ideas. However, if you are going to practise what you have learned from this book, then an equally important source of innovation will be your own ideas. The purpose of this final chapter is to help you to open up possibilities for developing your systemic work. We start with some ideas about an issue at the heart of a systems approach: creativity. Then we give examples of recent innovations in practice to illustrate the fact that there are endless unexplored possibilities awaiting your creativity. The third section reviews a research area as an indication of how we attempt to harness basic scientific information for practical purposes. Finally we show how the crucial task of monitoring your practice can be done effectively.

Creativity

At all levels, a systems approach places a premium on creativity. This does not just apply to the creation of hypotheses and interventions. Introducing systemic ideas into your workplace; making and maintaining a space that physically contributes to family therapy; freely shifting your observation between the family, the therapist, the video-recorder, the team, and yourself; writing appropriate letters to referrers; and many other tasks pose problems that require creative solutions.

One of the nice paradoxes about creativity is that since it is by definition unpredictable, it cannot be specified in advance. Yet there are things that can be done to make it more likely.

A fundamental condition for creativity is to feel in control of events. In panic, attention is narrowed, and we tend to do more of whatever has been our most common response. If panic increases we do the same thing only more so. So a condition for creativity is that we should establish an environment in which we feel safe. If you know that any idea you come up with will be met with derision and contempt, you are not likely to be able to think freely. Many of the ideas under 'Tools for us' in Chapter 7 can be seen as attempting to set up conditions in which energy will be directed to finding solutions (or problems) that break away from the tried and failed route.

Positive connotation is a powerful aid to creativity. By freeing us from dead-end solutions like blaming, and protecting us from a concentration on negatives, a consistent strategy of positive connotation becomes a remarkably pervasive influence. Specifically, when used consistently within a team, it completely prevents responses that shrivel initiative and focus people's energies on how to cope with their colleagues. O'Brian and Bruggen (1985) offer a creative and amusing account of how positive connotation could change your life.

Often, when you cannot find a solution it is because you have not started from a clear specification of the problem. If nothing that anyone can do will solve it, maybe 'it' is not a problem at all. Or maybe all the solutions are to a different problem. The technique of persistently asking 'what is the problem?' is certainly one that we can usefully apply to ourselves.

Often creativity depends on an ability to stand outside the issue in a way that corresponds to the systemic concept of 'going meta'. A broader perspective frees us from assumptions about what is or is not possible, or may help us to select an alternative goal which bypasses the obstacle.

Play is almost intrinsically creative, and a major route to thinking freely is to cultivate a playful attitude. There is a potential difficulty here because we are often dealing with issues that are not a laughing matter. However, a playful orientation does not have to trivialise or show disrespect. What it does is to refuse to accept the same posture of helplessness, antagonism, disapproval, or whatever it is that prevents the family from freely contemplating alternative perspectives. When someone in the team says 'this family survives by hating grandfather – what can we do to make them hate him even more, to the point that they start to worry about it?' there may be a burst of more and more outrageous suggestions. But at the end, when the laughter has died down, the team will be in a mood, and a position, to free themselves from the family's perceptions, and judge what the family might really be asked to do that would disrupt their current solution.

Creativity is not an end in itself for therapists, but a component of effective working. However, as Jenkins and Donnelly (1983) made clear, mobilizing the family's creativity should be an important objective. This consideration is part of the 'hunt the latitude' strategy (below) but considering the requirements for creativity that we have listed here should help give an indication both of why families may lose this capacity, and what needs to be done to help them regain it.

Finally, one technique that seems to be much more effective than it ought to be is to arrange for yourself to regularly receive the message 'be creative'. Quite often the response seems to be something like 'Oh yes, what a good idea' followed by a completely novel approach to the problem. It seems that people are often uncreative just because they forget to try.

Recent Innovations

The Reflexive Team

One relatively recent idea has been to make the process of family therapy reflexive. After some years of sitting behind one-way mirrors, family teams started to consider creatively that aspect of their work. You will by now be very familiar with the idea of reversing the accustomed direction of one's thinking as a way of breaking free of a fix. The first idea seems to have been to switch off the lights in the therapy room and turn them on in the team room so as to reverse the effect of the one-way mirror. Now the family could watch the team and could perhaps see in the team discussion a mirror of themselves. In our own work the first reversal came by inviting a member of the family to join the team behind the screen to observe the family and therapists. With later families we invited several members so that dyads or triads who were left in the therapy room could confront problems in a situation that they could not rely on the rest of the family to disrupt.

An example is a family in which the father had been excluded, by a coalition of mother and daughter. The younger (15 year old) son was classified as babyish, and any attempts at maturity were severely mocked. When the women in the family moved behind the screen, there was an immediate move by the son to engage father in a serious discussion of how he had coped with adolescence. Instantaneously the mother and daughter started making jokey but disparaging comments. Insulated from the interruption, father and son continued an emotional but constructive discussion with each trying hard to stay engaged and helpful. The attacks by the two women escalated for a while, until the team pointed out that something important was happening in the room, and that it might be useful to concentrate on trying to understand it.

What had become apparent in this episode was a well practised cycle by which problem solving communication was disrupted before it got under way. Family myths about the irrelevance of the father and the incapacity of the son were challenged in this episode, but the family style of an aggressive jokiness and disparagement could now be seen as a strategy by which all problems were avoided. Within the family the 'solution' worked so smoothly that we had not been able to recognise it until the barrier of the mirror, and the realignment of sub-systems made it apparent.

More recently, in common with other teams, we have recognised that family perceptions might be opened up more by seeing the process by which an hypothesis is formed, than by the end product. We have therefore taken sometimes to bringing the team discussion to the family by having the team enter the therapy room (after a careful context-setting exercise with the family) and conducting a discussion with the therapist while the family observes. In some settings the team remains with the family throughout the session, so that no part of their operation is conducted in isolation.

Anderson (1987) first formally proposed the idea of a *reflective* team as one way of reducing the hierarchical tendencies of hypothesising and bridging interventions. We have not accepted all of the strictures propounded by Anderson, and feel that the term 'reflexive' is more informative. The process of the team emerging from behind the screen can be seen as just one aspect of systemic therapists taking seriously what they claim about the construction and toleration of alternative stories. Therapist teams expose themselves to the family in a way that reciprocates the family's exposing itself to them; hypotheses are not constructed in a vacuum, safe from contradiction, but in the context (the perception of the family) in which they must function. The team, in other words, is exposed to the consequences of its own mode of functioning, and can therefore be expected to be guided towards a form of functioning that incorporates, but is still not controlled by, the family's understanding. A systems approach is intrinsically reflexive in that the methods used to help families are continually applied to the operation of the therapeutic team. In this sense, the reflective team is just one of the more recent manifestations of reflexivity. However in practice, this method of working does have a substantial impact in making a team more likely to be aware of systemic processes in its own functioning, and so probably justifies a label which indicates the fact that it is applying its perceptions to itself.

It is easy for novel strategies to be operated as gimmicks and as such they could quite possibly have useful effects so long as the team remained excited about them. However we know that such fads become progressively dysfunctional as the novelty wears off. We are offering the idea of the reflexive team because it makes sense in terms of the overall understanding we have of how systemic family therapy works. In one form or another, it seems likely to become one aspect of the standard range of options available.

Shadowing

A second recent departure has been to allocate a team member to one of the family during a session. There are various ways in which this can be done, and it has parallels with shadowing as used in role-play. The effects that are sought are that the shadow acquires a much more direct appreciation of the experiences of the allocated family member, and that the family member can use their shadow to break free from family injunctions not to mention certain issues.

An example of this technique was with the family of a twenty two year-old anorexic woman, the oldest daughter in a family of five. We had tried over several sessions to obtain open discussion, and the family seemed to be trying to cooperate. However, the parents continually told their daughter to say whatever she wanted, and somehow this usually operates as a warning that communication is not free of risk. We discussed the idea of shadowing the daughter with the family at one session, and they agreed to try it next time. One of the team spent twenty minutes with the daughter and then came into the session taking her chair, while she joined the team behind the screen. The discussion had been of the kinds of thing that she wanted to say to her parents but did not feel able to. The therapist then played 'the daughter if she had felt able to say everything she wanted'. While the therapist was discussing 'her' feelings with the family the daughter had control of the ear bug in case she wanted to correct or add to what the therapist was saying.

In fact there was nothing obviously problematic in what the daughter wanted to say at that stage, much of it having to do with not being able to show her love for her parents freely and be sure of their response. She also wanted them to find ways of showing they were still concerned about her without being intrusive and dominating. Considering some of the other issues that had been discussed quite freely in the previous sessions, this material seemed quite minor and yet there was a tremendous sense of release and freedom in the family when this phase was over, and the daughter replaced the therapist. Such exercises make it entirely clear that families have their own perceptions that it is very difficult to share. They remind us that all of our assumptions about how family members will think must be treated with great caution.

Hunt the Latitude

Taking a concept from attachment theory (Stratton, 1988b) the idea is to discover those areas in which the family have room for manoeuvre. Bowlby's (1982) account of attachment has at its heart the idea that the attachment process is intended to mobilise caregiving so that a young child's essential needs will be met. Once this process has been satisfactorily completed the child is freed to play, to explore, and to learn; in other words, to develop. We have called this state, in which needs have been met and the individual has resources to spare, a state of 'latitude' (see Hanks and Stratton, 1988 for a more detailed discussion). The general precondition for latitude is a secure base (Bowlby, 1988), but in any person's life there will be areas of security in which they can develop, and areas of insecurity when all of their energies are likely to be devoted to getting their own needs met.

Unless they are totally overwhelmed, rather than just stuck, a family will have areas in which there is latitude. One aspect of such an area is that people feel safe, so establishing the freedom that a playful orientation confers may only be possible through the process of establishing a reasonable degree of trust. Once this is achieved, the recognised area of latitude can be entered to enable the family to take risks such as discussing secrets, considering alternatives, thinking about the future and so on.

A very general perspective on therapy is that it must establish areas in which sufficient caregiving can be set up to give the client(s) latitude to develop. Systemic consultation is not usually trying to provide caregiving during the session, but to enable family members to care for each other. This is achieved by providing them with alternative stories, alternative ways of understanding, by which they are able to perceive the needs of others in the family, and perceive themselves as wanting to, and being able to, meet some of those needs.

Causal Beliefs and Research

You will by now have become familiar with our understanding of how families get trapped in unproductive cycles of functioning. Fundamental to this understanding is the notion that the perceptions of causality held by family members are powerful factors in the process. Correspondingly, much of therapy can be seen as an attempt to reverse some aspect of a family's causal beliefs. Almost invariably, if the symptom comes to be seen as a consequence of problems in the family and not just a cause of problems, we have opened up possibilities for movement. As we have been attending particularly to family members' beliefs about causes we have discovered that recording the beliefs is a powerful way of understanding what is going on in the family. For some time the research group at LFTRC has been working on systems to identify and analyse causal beliefs.

As an example of the kind of uses we can make of this research,we have found that mothers of abused children perceive their children as having much more control over events than they do. Also while mothers see the causes of negative events as coming from outside to affect them, they see the causes as likely to come from within the child (Stratton and Swaffer, 1988). Such a perception makes the child, and not the parent, responsible when things go wrong, and the pattern is one in which it is intrinsic characteristics of the child that are responsible. Our recent work indicates that this blaming pattern occurs whenever there is a poor relationship between parent and child, and other research suggests that it may apply also to poor marital relationships. Full details of the coding system and its applications are given in Stratton, Munton, Hanks, Heard and Davidson (1988).

We are making two points here: first, that any family worker might find it useful to pay particular attention to the patterns of family members' beliefs about the causes of significant events; and secondly, that it is not enough to have good ideas – the ideas need to be researched if we are to get the full benefit from them.

Systemic family therapy had its origins in a research enterprise that was not started with anything like family therapy in mind (see Chapter 1). It is surprising and disappointing that a field which has come to put the highest value on curiosity in its practice should have inspired so little basic research. Perhaps the excitement of therapy combined with pressure of need from families and referrers has really made most family therapists 'too busy' (Calam and Elliott, 1987). Or Cecchin (1989) may be right to claim that although researchers start out wanting to discover something, they become engrossed in the process of research itself and lose sight of what it is for. Whatever the reason for the neglect of research, it is unfortunate. Being engaged in research cultivates the wider perspective and the detailed curiosity about precisely how events are manifested, and the patterns they take, that are fundamental to a systemic approach.

Research can take many forms and the scale can be highly varied. Any information gathered under known conditions, and with some degree of generalisability can be the basis of research. Our perception is that for family therapy to continue to progress it is essential that it should develop a solid research base. Every practitioner could potentially contribute to this objective, and we think all would benefit personally from the experience. Like the therapy itself, research can be done successfully by individuals but if you can get a team together it is more likely to be fun, to be significant and to be completed.

Systemic Monitoring of Systemic Consultations

Evaluation often appears to be regarded as a daunting, if not frightening, prospect. However, the core concepts used in systemic practice may be turned to the purposes of evaluation. It does not require different skills but, rather, a model which may act as a framework to guide practitioners and trainers through the process.

In our view practitioners and trainers have an obligation to appraise their effectiveness, to answer how their work is helpful, in what circumstances, to whom, and for how long. Rather than relying upon anecdotal impressions and idealised notions of, in this case, family therapy being 'a good thing', or upon personal preferences and convictions, the demand now is for evidence. Moreover, whilst the prospect of 'failure' might deter would-be evaluators, this may be reframed as information which contributes to the development of practice and teaching. Put another way, evaluation is essential if practice and training are to be open systems, characterised by development and change based on the exchange of information.

There are two keys to effective evaluation. First, it should not be seen as a postscript to practice or training but an integral, central feature from the outset. If not incorporated from the beginning, much potentially vital information with which to assess change or the lack of it will have been lost. The second key is specificity: having aims, and objectives which together add up to realistic, clear answers to the fundamental question 'what . . .' in behavioural, cognitive and emotional terms, and lend themselves to indicators with which to monitor movement towards or away from the objectives. This description corresponds to the basic definition of a goal seeking system (Chapter 1). As a reminder, the requirements for effective functioning are:

1) To know what the goal is.
2) To have some measure of distance from the goal.
3) To have a process by which actions that reduce the distance from the goal become more frequent.

In their work with families or organisations systemic therapists look for both first and second order change. This approach is based on evidence which suggests that first order change, being difference and improvement in symptomatic complaints, will be more likely to endure if accompanied by change in the system's relationships and context, second order change (Bennun, 1986). A similar dual focus is indicated for trainers and for the recipients of training courses. First order change here centres on identifying the skills and concepts to be taught and acquired, measuring a before and after situation. Second order change focuses on the extent of change in practice or training as a result of involvement in a training exercise and the acquisition and retention of skills which consolidate strengths and confront gaps.

On the basis of this understanding it is possible to apply a model which has been devised for evaluating the effectiveness of practice and training (Preston-Shoot and Williams, 1987):

Step One: What is the current situation? What is required here, when evaluating practice, is a hypothesis which answers the key questions: what is happening; what is maintaining this; what is its meaning, function or purpose; what makes it problematic now (Lask, 1980)? For members of a training course, the requirement here is to identify the skills and knowledge they bring to the course; their expectations, strengths and gaps in understanding and practice; their experience and fearful fantasies of the course and method of working; what they are hoping to learn. For trainers, the challenge is to identify the content and process of the course, both generally and in its component parts. These hypotheses, statements and formulations should indicate:

Step Two: What is the desired situation? When evaluating practice, this means identifying the change people are seeking and/or will settle for. For trainers and course members, it marks a hoped-for end-point: course content communicated; a process which has facilitated rather than impeded learning; skills and knowledge learned; expectations fulfilled.

Step Three: What are the objectives? This step requires that the desired situation is 'broken down' or teased out further into its component parts. This will then indicate:

Step Four: What is the plan? This is how practitioners and trainers intend to achieve the objectives and desired situation which they have specified. The 'how' should be clearly linked to the previous steps and the hypotheses which underpin them. The elements of the plan should, also, be realistic and achievable. In other words, the requirements are the same as for tasks and rituals used in interventions.

Step Five: What indicators will be used to indicate movement towards or away from the desired situation and objectives? What mechanisms exist to ensure that this information feeds back to influence practice?

Step Six: Review. When evaluating practice outcomes, the key questions are: what changes have occurred in the symptom; have new problems arisen or has the original problem reappeared in a different form; what changes have there been in relationships within the system being worked with; have the goals been achieved (Lask, 1980)? Trainers evaluate course outcomes both in terms of content and process: was the content communicated; how was it perceived; were the objectives of the trainer and course achieved; if so, what facilitated this; if not, what obstructed the process? Similarly, course members may assess what they have learned; the extent to which their practice, and their confidence within it, has evolved; whether and to what extent their objectives have been met; what facilitated or impeded their learning; what goals now appear appropriate for their practice and learning.

The tools for providing specific information with which to 'flesh out' steps one, two and three, and to provide evidence of movement during reviews, include the use of sentence completion, self-reports, observation by peers and supervisors, rating scales, circular questioning ,and questionnaires (for examples, see Preston-Shoot 1987; Preston-Shoot, 1988). The key, once again, is specificity: questions which will elicit differences in behaviour, perceptions, and beliefs, and which will enable clear statements about what has/has not changed.

Bibliography

Adams, R. and Hill, G. (1983) The labours of Hercules: some good reasons why social workers should not try to be different and practise family therapy. *Journal of Family Therapy,* **5 (1)**, 71–80.

Addison, C. (1982) A defence against the public? Aspects of intake in a social services department. *British Journal of Social Work,* **12 (6)**, 605–18.

Anderson, T. (1987) The reflecting team: dialogue and meta-dialogue in clinical work. *Family Process,* **26**, 415–28.

Bateson, G. (1973) *Steps to an Ecology of Mind.* St. Albans: Paladin.

Becvar, D. S. and Becvar, R. J. (1988) *Family Therapy, A Systemic Integration.* Boston: Allyn and Bacon.

Bennun, I. (1986) Evaluating family therapy: a comparison of the Milan and problem solving approaches. *Journal of Family Therapy,* **8 (3)**, 235–42.

Bentovim, A. and Gilmour, L. (1981) A family therapy interactional approach to decision making in child care, access and custody cases... *Journal of Family Therapy,* **3 (2)**, 65–77.

Bentovim, A., Elton, A., Hildebrand, J., Tranter, M., and Vizard, E. (1988) *Child Sexual Abuse Within The Family.* London: Wright.

Blackler, F. and Shimmin, S. (1984) *Applying Psychology In Organisations.* London: Methuen.

Blom-Cooper, L. (1988) A patch for a punctured ideal. *Social Services Insight,* **3 (18)**, 12–14.

Boscolo, L., Cecchin, G., Campbell, D. and Draper, R. (1985) Twenty more questions. In: *Applications of Systemic Family Therapy* (eds D. Campbell and R. Draper) London: Grune and Stratton.

Boscolo, L., Cecchin, G., Hoffman, L., and Penn, P. (1987) *Milan Systemic Family Therapy.* New York: Basic Books.

Bowlby, J. (1982) *Attachment* (2nd Ed.) New York: Basic Books.

Bowlby, J. (1988) *A Secure Base.* London: Tavistock.

Braye, S. and Preston-Shoot, M. (1990) On teaching and applying the law in social work: it is not that simple. *British Journal of Social Work,* **20 (4)**, 333–53.

Burnham, J. and Harris, Q. (1988) Systemic family therapy: the Milan approach. In: *Family Therapy in Britain* (eds E. Street and W. Dryden). Milton Keynes: Open University Press.

Byng-Hall, J. (1985) The family script: A useful bridge between theory and practice. *Journal of Family Therapy,* **7 (3)**, 301–305.

Byng-Hall, J. (1986) Family scripts: A concept which can bridge child psychotherapy and family therapy thinking. *Journal of Child Psychotherapy*, **12,** 3–13.

Byng-Hall, J. (1988) Scripts and legends in families and family therapy. *Family Process*, **27**, 167–79.

Byng-Hall, J. and Campbell, D. (1981) Resolving conflicts in family distance regulation: an integrative approach. *Journal of Marital and Family Therapy*, **7**, 321–30.

Cade, B. and Cornwell, M. (1985) New realities for old: Some uses of teams and one-way screens in therapy. In: *Applications of Systemic Family Therapy*. (Eds D. Campbell and R. Draper.) London: Grune and Stratton.

Calam, R. M. and Elliott, P. A. (1987) Why are we 'too busy'? Problems of practitioner research in family therapy. *Journal of Family Therapy*, **9 (4)**, 329–37.

Campbell, D. and Draper, R. (eds) (1985) *Applications of Systemic Family Therapy: The Milan Approach*. London: Grune and Stratton.

Carl, D. and Jurkovic, G. (1983) Agency triangles: problems in agency-family relationships. *Family Process*, **22**, 441–51.

Carter, B. and McGoldrick, M. (1989) *The Changing Family Life Cycle*. (2nd Ed.) Massachusetts: Allyn and Bacon.

Casement, P. (1985) *On Learning From the Patient*. London: Tavistock.

Cecchin, G. (1987) Hypothesising, circularity and neutrality revisited: an invitation to curiosity. *Family Process*, **26 (4)**, 405–13.

Cecchin, G. (1989) Recorded discussion at Kensington Consultation Centre, London.

Corden, J. and Preston-Shoot, M. (1987) *Contracts In Social Work*. Aldershot: Gower.

Coulshed, V. and Abdullah-Zadeh, J. (1983) The family as a unit of treatment: a case record. *British Journal of Social Work*, **13 (1)**, 39–55.

Coulshed, V. and Abdullah-Zadeh, J. (1985) The side effects of intervention? *British Journal of Social Work*, **15 (5)**, 479–86.

Currie, P., Evans, E. and Oliver, X. (1988) The suitcase syndrome. *Social Work Today*, **20 (9)**, 22–3.

Dare, C. (1979) Psychoanalysis and systems in family therapy. *Journal of Family Therapy*, **1 (2)**, 137–51.

de Shazar, S. (1986) *Keys to Solution in Brief Family Therapy*. London: W. W. Norton.

Dell, P. F. (1989) Violence and the systemic view: the problem of power. *Family Process*, **25**, 513–21.

Dimmock, B. and Dungworth, D. (1983) Creating manoeuvrability for family/systems therapists in social services departments. *Journal of Family Therapy*, **5 (1)**, 53–69.

Dimmock, B. and Dungworth, D. (1985) Beyond the family: using network meetings with statutory child care cases. *Journal of Family Therapy*, **7 (1)**, 45–68.

Dowling, E. (1979) Co-therapy: a clinical researcher's view. In: *Family and Marital Psychotherapy* (ed. S. Walrond-Skinner). London: RKP.

Dungworth, D. (1988) Context and the construction of family therapy practice. In: *Family Therapy in Britain.* (Eds E. Street and W. Dryden). Milton Keynes: Open University Press.

Dungworth, D. and Reimers, S. (1984) Family therapy in social services departments. In: *Using Family Therapy.* (Eds. A. Treacher and J. Carpenter). Oxford: Basil Blackwell.

Evans, R. (1976) Some implications of an integrated model of social work for theory and practice. *British Journal of Social Work,* **6 (2)**, 177–200.

Family Service Units (1982) *Family Involvement In the Social Work Process.* London: Family Service Units.

Ferreira, A. J. (1963) Family myth and homeostasis. *Archives of General Psychiatry,* **9**, 457–63.

Fisch, R. Weakland, J. H., and Segal, L. (1982) *Tactics of Change.* California: Jossey-Bass.

Fish, V. (1990) Introducing causality and power into family therapy theory: A correction to the systemic paradigm. *Journal of Marital and Family Therapy,* **16**, 21–37.

Francis, M. (1988) The skeleton in the cupboard: experiential geneogram work for family therapy trainees. *Journal of Family Therapy,* **10 (2)**, 135–52.

Furniss, T. (1983a) Family process in the treatment of intrafamilial child sexual abuse. *Journal of Family Therapy,* **5 (4)**, 263–8.

Furniss, T. (1983b) Mutual influence and interlocking professional-family process in the treatment of child sexual abuse and incest. *Child Abuse and Neglect,* **7**, 207–23.

Glaser, D. and Frosh, S. (1988) *Child Sexual Abuse.* London: Macmillan.

Haley, J. (1963) *Strategies of Psychotherapy.* New York: Grune and Stratton.

Hanks, H. G. I. and Stratton, P. M. (1988) Family perspectives on early sexual abuse. In: *Early Prediction and Prevention of Child Abuse.* (Eds. K. Browne, C. Davies and P. M. Stratton). Chichester: Wiley.

Hare-Mustin, R. (1987) The problem of gender in family therapy theory. *Family Process,* **26**, 15–27.

Harris, N. (1987) Defensive social work. *British Journal of Social Work,* **17 (1)**, 61–69.

Heinl, P. (1985) The image and visual analysis of the geneogram. *Journal of Family Therapy,* **7 (3)**, 213–29.

Heinl, P. (1987) Interactional sculpt: examples from a training seminar. *Journal of Family Therapy,* **9 (2)**, 189–98.

Hoffman, L. (1981) *Foundations of Family Therapy.* New York: Basic Books.

Holdaway, S. (1986) Police and social work relations – problems and possibilities. *British Journal of Social Work,* **16 (2)**, 137–60.

Israelstam, K. (1988) Contrasting four major family therapy paradigms: Implications for family therapy training. *Journal of Family Therapy,* **10 (2)**, 179–94.

James, K. and MacKinnon, L. (1990) The incestuous family revisited:

a critical analysis of family therapy myths. *Journal of Marital and Family Therapy*, **16**, 71–88.

Jaques, E. (1955) Social systems as defence against persecutory and depressive anxiety. In: *New Directions In Psychoanalysis*. (Eds. M. Klein, P. Heimann and R. Money-Kyrle.) London: Tavistock.

Jenkins, H., and Donnelly, M. (1983) The therapists responsibility: a systemic approach to mobilizing family creativity. *Journal of Family Therapy*, **5 (3)**, 199–218.

Kingston, P. (1979) The social context of family therapy. In: *Family and Marital Psychotherapy*. (Ed. S. Walrond-Skinner.) London: RKP.

Kingston, P. and Smith, D. (1983) Preparation for live consultation and live supervision when working without a one-way screen. *Journal of Family Therapy*, **5 (3)**, 219–33.

L'Abate, L. (1985) *The Handbook of Family Psychology and Therapy*, Vols I & II. Chicago: Dorsey.

Lask, B. (1980) Evaluation – why and how? (a guide for clinicians). *Journal of Family Therapy*, **2 (2)**, 199–210.

Liddle, H. A. (1988) Systemic supervision: conceptual overlays and pragmatic guidelines. In: *Handbook of Family Therapy and Supervision*.(Eds H. A. Liddle, D. Breunlin and R. Schwartz.) New York: Guilford.

Lieberman, S. (1979) Transgenerational analysis: the geneogram as a technique in family therapy. *Journal of Family Therapy*, **1 (1)**, 51–64.

Malan, D. (1979) *Individual Psychotherapy and the Science of Psychodynamics*. London: Butterworths.

Mason, B. (1986) Neutrality: the worker and family therapy. In: *Skills for Social Workers in the 80's*. (Eds. M. Marshall, M. Preston-Shoot and E. Wincott.) Birmingham: British Association of Social Workers.

Mattinson, J. and Sinclair, I. (1979) *Mate and Stalemate*. Oxford: Basil Blackwell.

Menzies, I. (1970) *The Functioning Of Social Systems As A Defence Against Anxiety*. London: Tavistock.

Miller, J. and Cook, T. (eds) (1981) *Direct Work With Families*. London: Bedford Square Press.

Minuchin, S. (1974) *Families and Family Therapy*. London: Tavistock.

O'Brian, C. and Bruggen, P. (1985) Our personal and professional lives: learning positive connotation and circular questioning. *Family Process*, **24**, 311–22.

Palazzoli, M. Selvini, *see Selvini Palazzoli*.

Palmer, B. and McCaughan, N. (1988) All in a day's work. *Community Care*, 2nd June.

Papp, P. (1980) The Greek chorus and other techniques of paradoxical therapy. *Family Process*, **19**, 45–57.

Penn, P. (1982) Circular questioning. *Family Process*, **21 (3)**, 267–80.

Penn, P. (1985) Feed-forward: future questions, future maps. *Family Process*, **24 (3)**, 299–310.

Persaud, R. D. (1987) Effects of the one-way mirror in family therapy. *Journal of Family Therapy*, **9 (1)**, 75–79.

Piggin, L. and Watson, A. (1979) The decision to co-work. *FSU Quarterly*, **19**, 16–26.
Pilalis, J. and Anderton, J. (1986) Feminism and family therapy – a possible meeting point. *Journal of Family Therapy*, **8 (2)**, 99–114.
Pirrotta, S. and Cecchin, G. (1988) The Milan training program. In: *Handbook of Family Therapy Training and Supervision*. (Eds H. A. Liddle, D. Breunlin and R. Schwartz.) New York: Guilford.
Pottle, S. (1984) Developing a network-orientated service for elderly people and their carers. In: *Using Family Therapy*. (Eds A. Treacher and J. Carpenter.) Oxford: Basil Blackwell.
Preston-Shoot, M. (1987) *Effective Groupwork*. London: Macmillan.
Preston-Shoot, M. (1988) A model for evaluating groupwork. *Groupwork*, **1 (2)**, 147–57.
Preston-Shoot, M. and Agass, D. (1990) *Making Sense of Social Work: Psychodynamics, Systems And Practice*. London: Macmillan.
Preston-Shoot, M. and Williams, J. (1987) A model for evaluating the effectiveness of practice. *Practice*, **1 (4)**, 393–405.
Reay, R. (1986) Bridging the gap: a model for integrating theory and practice. *British Journal of Social Work*, **16 (1)**, 49–64.
Reder, P. (1986) Multiagency family systems. *Journal of Family Therapy*, **8 (2)**, 139–52.
Reder, P. (1988) 'Because': a suggested contribution to systemic and strategic therapy. *Journal of Family Therapy*, **10 (1)**, 75–81.
Segal, L. (1986) *The Dream of Reality*. New York: Norton.
Selvini Palazzoli, M., Boscolo, L., Cecchin, G. and Prata, G. (1978) *Paradox And Counterparadox*. New York: Jason Aronson.
Selvini Palazzoli, M., Boscolo, L., Cecchin, G. and Prata, G. (1980a) Hypothesising – circularity – neutrality: three guidelines for the conductor of the session. *Family Process*, **19 (1)**, 3–12.
Selvini Palazzoli, M., Boscolo, L., Cecchin, G. and Prata, G. (1980b) The problem of the referring person. *Journal of Marital and Family Therapy*, **6**, 3–9.
Selvini Palazzoli, M., Anolli, L., Pisano, I., Ricci, C., Sacchi, M. and Ugazio, V. (1987) *The Hidden Games of Organisations*. New York: Pantheon.
Shotter, J. and Gergen, K. J. (1989) *Texts of Identity*. London: Sage.
Sluzki, C. and Ransom, D. (1976) *Double Bind: The Foundation of the Communicational Approach to the Family*. London: Grune and Stratton.
Smith, D. and Kingston, P. (1980) Live supervision without a one-way screen. *Journal of Family Therapy*, **2 (4)**, 379–87.
Specht, H. and Vickery, A. (eds) (1977) *Integrating Social Work Methods*. London: George Allen and Unwin.
Stevenson, O. (1986) Guest editorial on the Jasmine Beckford Inquiry. *British Journal of Social Work*, **16 (5)**, 501–10.
Stevenson, O. (1988) Law and social work education: a commentary on 'The Law Report'. *Issues In Social Work Education*, **8 (1)**, 37–45.
Stratton, P. M. (1982) *Psychobiology of the Human Newborn*. Chichester: Wiley.
Stratton, P. M. (1988a) Parents' conceptualization of children as the

organizer of culturally structured environments. In: *Child Development Within Culturally Structured Environments.* (Ed. J. Valsiner.) Norwood, New Jersey: Abbx. 5–29.

Stratton, P. M. (1988b) Spirals and circles: Potential contributions of developmental psychology to family therapy. *Journal of Family Therapy*, **10 (3)**, 207–31.

Stratton, P. M. and Swaffer, R. (1988) Maternal causal beliefs for abused and handicapped children. *Journal of Reproductive and Infant Psychology*, **6**, 201–16.

Stratton, P. M., Davies, C. and Browne, K. (1988) The psychological context of child abuse and neglect. In: *Early Prediction and Prevention of Child Abuse and Neglect.* (Eds K. Browne, C. Davies and P. M. Stratton.) Chichester: Wiley. pp 291–302.

Stratton, P. M., Munton, A. G., Hanks, H. G. I., Heard, D. H. and Davidson, C. (1988), *Leeds Attributional Coding System (LACS) Manual.* pp 1–133. Leeds: Leeds Family Therapy and Research Centre.

Street, E. (1981) The family therapist and staff-group consultancy. *Journal of Family Therapy*, **3 (2)**, 187–99.

Summit, R. (1983) The child sexual abuse accommodation syndrome. *Child Abuse and Neglect*, **7**, 177–93.

Tomm, K. (1984) One perspective on the Milan systemic approach: part 1: overview of development, theory and practice. *Journal of Marital and Family Therapy*, **10 (2)**, 113–25.

Treacher, A. (1986) Invisible patients, invisible families – a critical exploration of some technocratic trends in family therapy. *Journal of Family Therapy*, **8 (3)**, 267–306.

Treacher, A. and Carpenter, J. (eds) (1984) *Using Family Therapy.* Oxford: Basil Blackwell.

Walrond-Skinner, S. (1976) *Family Therapy: The Treatment of Natural Systems.* London: RKP.

Walsh, F. (1982) *Normal Family Processes.* New York: Guilford.

Watzlawick, P., Beavin, J. and Jackson, D. (1967) *Pragmatics of Human Communication.* New York: Norton.

Whittington, C. (1977) Social workers' orientations: an action perspective. *British Journal of Social Work*, **7 (1)**, 73–95.

Wilkinson, I. (1987) Family Assessment: A review. *Journal of Family Therapy*, **9 (4)**, 367–80.

Williams, J. and Watson, G. (1988) Sexual inequality, family life and family therapy. In: *Family Therapy In Britain.* (Eds E. Street and W. Dryden.) Milton Keynes: Open University Press.

Williams, M. (1966) Limitations, fantasies and security operations of beginning group psychotherapists. *International Journal of Group Psychotherapy*, **16**, 150–62.

Wynne, L., McDaniel, S. H. and Weber, T. T. (1987) Professional politics and the concepts of family therapy, family consultation, and systems consultation. *Family Process*, **26**, 153–66.

Index

Absent members 35
Accommodation syndrome 133
Adolescent units 109
Adoptive parents 138
Alternative perspectives 3, 11, 75, 79
Alternative stories 18, 67–8, 143, 144
Anxieties 30, 100, 124, 127
Anorexia 14, 143
Assessment 115, 123
Assessment sessions 31, 34–8
Attachment theory 144

Beliefs 20–1, 38, 83–6, 116, 138, 145
Binds 18, 121, 133
Boundaries 14, 32, 38, 87, 90, 109, 118, 120–1, 132
Bridging interventions 59, 63, 70, 71–81, 82, 84, 143
  counter-paradox 77–8
  making the symptom worse 76–7
  prescribing the symptom 77
  presenting the hypothesis 75–6
  take away the constraints 74
  take away the mutual support 75

Casual beliefs 145–6
Causal connections 16, 132
Casuality 16, 115
  reversal of 83
Causes 24
Child abuse 4, 65, 96, 98, 107, 110, 121, 123, 131–9
Circles/Circularity 23–8, 42, 44, 49, 57, 131, 137
Circular questions 34, 35, 44, 51–4, 57, 69, 81, 118, 127
Circular questioning 41, 51–4, 63, 100, 139, 148
Closed systems 97, 102, 119
Closure 44, 122
Co-working 101–3
Collusion 115
Communication 13, 14, 30, 60, 68, 120–1, 123
Complementarity 25, 65, 72, 97
Compulsion 35, 110
Consultant 85, 101, 119, 120, 129
Contracts 36, 124
Countertransference 30, 97
Creativity 140–1
Culture 17, 20
Curiosity 44, 65, 66, 102, 111, 129, 145

Day hospitals 109
Defence mechanisms 97, 124

Defences 30, 99
Defensive practice 98, 113, 123, 124
Defining the problem 54–6, 67
Delivering interventions 80
Detoured conflict 48, 50, 86, 115, 125
Detouring problems 66
Detouring responsibility 126
Differences 11
Distance regulator 48, 132, 135
Double binds 22–3, 28, 60, 61, 78, 137

Earbug/earpiece 33, 94, 101
Economic/social systems 112–3
Enmeshed 31, 46, 51, 61, 102, 114, 121, 126, 136
Escalation 25, 26, 97, 125
Evaluation 146–8

Failing to thrive 131–6
Family 8, 15–28
Family-agency interaction 29–40, 114–5
Family-worker interaction 29–40, 115–6
Family history 20
Family structure 38
First order change 146–7
Foster parents 138

Gender/gender roles 83, 89, 111–2
Geneograms 30, 38–40, 82, 89–92, 109, 118, 121, 133–4
Goal seeking 12–3, 146
Going meta 61, 126–7, 131, 141
Groups 136

Hierarchies 38
Hunt the latitude 141, 144–5
Hypotheses 29, 30, 35–7, 59, 62, 63, 65, 69, 73, 81–3, 139, 147
Hypothesising 32, 38, 41–58, 101, 109, 118, 126, 143

Indentity 19–20
Incest 87, 131
Indicators for therapy 34–5
Individual functioning15–7
Internal supervisor 44, 102
Interventions 30, 33, 34, 41, 46, 59–70, 72, 101, 115, 118, 133

Law/legal duties 111–3
Leeds Family Therapy and Research Centre 3, 6, 14, 145
Leverage 46, 49, 62, 66, 76, 93, 125
Life cycle 17, 29, 41, 46

Linear punctuations 24, 25, 42, 44, 45, 46, 51, 54, 63, 86, 110–1, 119, 129
Live supervision 101, 109

Meta 49, 56, 61, 72, 103
Metacommunication 60–2, 68, 73, 123
Meta perspective 44, 61, 94, 126, 129
Meta position 5, 51, 88, 115, 129, 133, 137
Meta view 36, 45–6, 100, 101
Metaphors 41
Mirroring 82, 87–8, 99, 102, 118, 126, 128, 136
Monitoring 146–8
More of the same 18–9, 26, 124, 133
Myths 21, 38, 46, 57, 82, 83–6, 90, 91, 96, 120, 123, 138

Naming the game 66–7, 69, 74, 75
Negative connotation 42
Negative feedback 12
Neutrality 31, 42, 44, 45, 49, 51, 56, 64–6, 72, 110–1, 129, 131, 133, 136, 137, 139
'No change' prescription 77
No shocks/No weakness 20, 124–5
Non-verbal communication 60

Objections 109–13
One down 54, 93, 142
One-way mirror 33, 36, 100–1

Patterns 38, 40, 66, 90, 96
Perceptions 17, 24, 51, 63, 65, 68, 72, 91
Perspective 15, 23, 43, 51, 52, 111, 123
Play/playfulness 44, 141, 144
Positive connotation 9, 29, 42, 44, 48, 53, 62, 63–4, 72, 88, 94, 116, 127, 131, 132, 141
Positive feedback 13
Power 17, 20, 104, 111–2, 132
Practice dilemmas 98–9, 113, 124
Process interventions 59–70
Professionals' meetings 31–4, 122–3, 134–5
Professional systems 31, 85, 99, 118–30, 132, 135
as part of the problem 98, 113
Psychodynamic psychotherapy 44, 87
Punctuation 23–8, 46, 51, 54, 89, 97, 121–3, 126

Reciprocal sequences 25
Recording 101
Redundant solutions 27, 73, 109, 119
Referral games 31, 114, 125
Referrals 29–40, 46, 113
Reflexive team 142–3
Reframing 63–4, 69, 78, 116, 117, 146
Research 145–6
Residential settings 109
Review 34, 103, 148
Rituals 38, 71, 76
Role-plays 4–5
Roles in team 101–4

Scapegoating 121, 132
Schizophrenia 13
Scripts 5, 21–2, 46, 51, 57, 83–6, 96, 97, 98, 102, 112, 113, 116, 118, 121–3, 125, 126, 129
Sculpts 51, 92–3, 118
Second order change 146–7
Secretary 35, 80
Secrets 8, 18, 38, 59, 66, 67, 89, 90, 123, 126
Self-awareness 38, 96–7
Self-scrutiny 44
Session trips 56–7
Sexual abuse 59, 89, 97, 122, 125, 136–9
Shadowing 143–4
Sibling groups 138–9
Social constructions 12, 112
Social services 109, 120
Solutions 10, 15, 18–9, 26, 29, 49, 72, 113, 123, 142
Spirals 26, 42, 44, 90, 132, 136, 138
Splitting the team 67, 69
Statutory work 110–1, 127
Strategic family therapy 14, 60
Structural family therapy 14, 87, 89
Structural inequalities 112, 125
Stuck/stuckness 3, 10, 23, 24, 29, 46, 51, 54–5, 57, 66, 77, 88, 101, 113, 128, 137
Supervision 5, 36, 95, 96–105, 120, 148
Supervisory viewpoint 126, 129
Support groups 116
Symmetry 16, 26, 43, 50, 68, 71, 113, 136
Systemic approach 3, 4, 7–14

Teaching 3
Teams/teamworking 33, 36, 59, 88, 90, 91, 93–5, 120, 127
Therapeutic alliance 30, 91
Therapeutic objectives 68
Therapist manoeuvrability 42, 46, 56, 66, 120
Therapist's tools 82–95
Too far - too close 50
Tools for action 82, 91–3
Tools for understanding 82–91
Tools for us 82, 93–5, 116–7, 140
Trainers 4–5, 146
Training 5, 36, 53, 97, 102, 123, 146–8
Transactions 24, 113
Transference 30, 97
Trial identifications 44
Triangles 82, 86–7, 89, 109
Triangulation 31, 48, 50, 86–7, 99, 114, 121, 125

Video 33, 35, 36, 59
Voluntary agencies 109

Ways of working 34, 128
What is the problem 54–6, 114, 128, 141
Working agreements 110, 114